Presenting the Past

1

Britain 1066–1500

Tony McAleavy
Andrew Wrenn
Keith Worrall

Collins

Contents

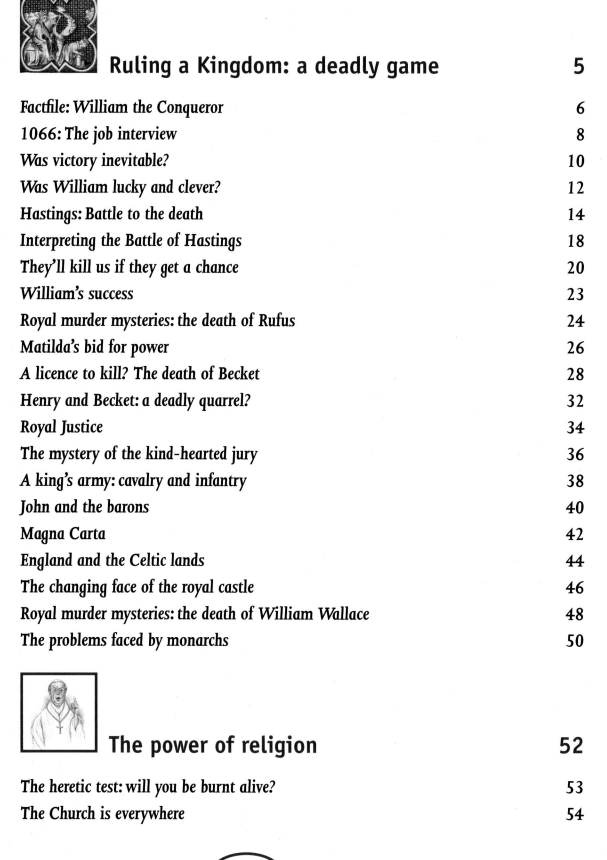

Medieval people: did they have a hard life? 79

Published by Collins Educational
An imprint of HarperCollins*Publishers* Limited
77–85 Fulham Palace Road
Hammersmith
London
W6 8JB

www.**Collins**Education.com
On-line support for schools and colleges

British Library Cataloguing in Publication Data
A catalogue record for this publication is available
from the British Library.

Edited by Susannah Baccardax and Samantha Davey
Design by Ken Vail Graphic Design, Cambridge
Cover design by Derek Lee
Artwork by Peter Bull
Picture research by Samantha Davey
Production by Kathryn Botterill
Printed and bound by Printing Express Limited in Hong Kong

Ruling a kingdom: a deadly game

In the Middle Ages kings and queens were playing a deadly game. If they did well, they won a life of wealth and luxury. If they did badly, they could be overthrown and killed. The chance of losing was high.
There were twenty kings of England between 1066 and 1500. Seven of them died violently.

The prize for the winners: great wealth   **The penalty for the losers: death**

Why did some win and some lose? The first section of this book is all about kings and queens and the problems they faced. Some kings and queens did well; we say they were **successful**. Others couldn't cope with their problems; they were **unsuccessful**. As you find out more about the lives of kings and queens, think about why some were more successful than others.

---

1 Look at this information about four kings. Which ones were successful and which ones were unsuccessful?

◆ **Edward I** fought and won many battles and conquered Wales. He died peacefully.

◆ **Edward II** was defeated in war by the Scots. He was later murdered by his own wife.

◆ **Richard III** was killed in battle by another man who wanted to be king.

◆ **Edward III** was seen as a great hero for his victories in war against the French. He died peacefully.

Can you spot a reason why some of these kings were successful?

Factfile: William the Conqueror

William the Conqueror ruled England from 1066 to 1087. He was one of the most successful kings of England. This factfile gives you information on William's life before he became king. You can find out what sort of a person he was and why he was so successful.

1 If you wanted to be a successful king in the Middle Ages do you think it was better to be:
   ◆ good at fighting
   ◆ tough with enemies
   ◆ good at making friends with people
   ◆ well educated

2 Look at the files about William. Which of the four phrases in question 1 describes William?

File 1: Occupation

Before becoming King of England, William was Duke of Normandy and ruled over the area of northern France called Normandy.

File 2: Childhood

William's father was the Duke of Normandy. His mother was from a much more ordinary family. His mother and father were not married and they split up shortly after he was born. William's father was very violent. He died when William was only 8 years old. William then became the new Duke of Normandy.

The next few years were very difficult for young William. There were many fights between noblemen. These nobles each had their own small army and they fought against each other. Many of William's close friends were killed in these fights. One of his supporters had his throat cut in William's bedroom. Living like this made William very tough. He distrusted most people. He decided that people would only obey him if he was strong and threatening.

File 3: Nickname

He was called William the Bastard. He did not like this nickname.

William talks to his brothers. Later he argued with one of them and put him in prison. Why do you think he holds a sword as he speaks?

File 4: Education

At this time hardly anyone went to school, so William was not taught to write. Only those who were going to work for the Church learnt to write. Instead of studying, William spent his time learning to be a soldier. He spent many hours each day practising horse riding and fighting.

File 5: Career

Once he was old enough, William began to make sure that everyone in Normandy did what he said. He set up an army to smash his enemies. This became one of the strongest armies in Europe. His knights were experts at winning battles by charging on their huge war-horses. With help from his army, William defeated his enemies over and over again. By 1066, William had an amazing record as a general (army leader): he had fought in many wars but had never lost a single battle.

File 6: Personality

William was hard-working. He was generous to a small group of his special friends as long as they did what he said. He was very strict with anyone who disobeyed him. He sentenced his own brother to life in prison after an argument. He was very cruel at times. In one war in Normandy, he attacked a town and captured some enemy soldiers. People in the town refused to surrender and shouted abuse at him from inside the town walls. His answer was to march thirty of the captured soldiers to the town walls and cut off their hands and feet. The horrified townsfolk surrendered immediately.

3 Here are six adjectives. Pick out three which describe William well and three which do not describe William:
   ◆ Clever   ◆ Likeable   ◆ Lazy   ◆ Fierce   ◆ Trusting   ◆ Brutal
   Explain your choices.

4 Using all the information you have found out about William's character, say why you think he was so successful.

William gives orders to his army from horseback. He is wearing a suit of chain-mail and is carrying a mace (club) which is a sign that he is in charge.

1066: The job interview

It was January 1066. Edward, the King of England had just died. Usually, one of the king's children would take over ruling the country, but Edward had no children. Harold Godwinson took over at first, but he had two rivals. Which of the three men had the best claim to be King of England?

The candidates:

◆ Harold Godwinson, a powerful English nobleman.

◆ Harald Hardrada, King of Norway and a famous Viking warrior.

◆ William, Duke of Normandy.

They all thought that they were the best candidate for the job of king. Each one was ready to fight for the crown of England.

Today when people go for a job they usually have an interview. Let us imagine that we could interview the three candidates who wanted to be king. We can ask them three questions to see whether they should be king. You've checked their answers and none of them are lying. Now you must decide who is best qualified to get the job. Look at the answers they give to each question and give them a mark out of 10.

Question 1: Royal blood

'The English expect that the new king will be a member of their royal family. Are you related to the royal family of England?'

Harold Godwinson

'Nearly. I have to admit, I'm not actually one of the royal family. But there is a link. My sister was the wife of the old king. I'm almost one of the family.'

10

Harald Hardrada

'No, but unlike the other two I'm a proper king already. I'm nothing to do with the royal family of England but I am the King of Norway.'

10

William

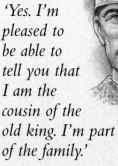

'Yes. I'm pleased to be able to tell you that I am the cousin of the old king. I'm part of the family.'

10

Question 2: The old king's choice

'We like a new king to be chosen by the old king before he dies. Did the last king, Edward, want you to take over as the next king?'

Harold Godwinson

'Yes he did. He also made some vague promise to William way back in 1051 but he soon changed his mind. Before he died, he clearly said that I must be the next king.' **10**

Harald Hardrada

'No he didn't, but years ago another English king promised my family that we could take over England one day.' **10**

William

'Yes he did. In 1051, Edward announced that I should take over from him if he had no children.' **10**

Question 3: Experience

'We need a king who can do the job well. Do you have the right experience to be a good king of England?'

Harold Godwinson

'I've already been running the country successfully for years. I'm sorry to say that the old king was rather lazy. I was his deputy and I did all the real work. I think he was training me so that I could take over when he died. I've organised the government and the army and it's all gone very well.' **10**

Harald Hardrada

'I've been King of Norway for many years. Most of the time I'm away from home fighting. When I'm home my main job is getting enough money from people to pay for my next war. I don't know why but the people of Norway seem to hate me. They call me Harald the Bad.' **10**

William

'Look what I've already done in Normandy. When I became Duke it was in a mess. There was lots of fighting and crime. I sorted it out by being tough on criminals and law-breakers. I'd do the same as King of England.' **10**

You Decide

1 Add up your scores for each candidate and put them in rank order.

2 Take the candidate with the highest score and explain why you think they are best suited for the job.

3 Write a short letter to the other two candidates explaining why they didn't get the job.

Was victory inevitable?

Being the most suitable person for the job was no guarantee of success. In 1066 such problems were usually settled by force. The winner had to defeat his rivals in battle to become king. Hardrada and William both invaded England with their armies to try to win the crown from Harold.

Was it **inevitable** (bound to happen) that William would be successful? He faced some serious problems that he had to overcome before he could become king. It was not an easy task.

---

1 From what you know already do you think that William was bound to win before the fighting started?

2 Look at the problems faced by William. For each problem say why it made it more difficult for him to win.

3 Using the information on these pages explain whether William was bound to win.

William's 1st problem: His rivals had won many battles.

His two rivals were both very good generals. Harold Godwinson had years of experience of fighting. In 1063, for example, he led an army that defeated the people of Wales. Harald Hardrada was the most famous Viking fighter of the time. He was very difficult to beat (his second name means 'hard ruler'). He had spent many years as a successful soldier in several different countries.

Both of William's rivals had very fierce soldiers to help them. The picture on this page shows some of the soldiers of Harold Godwinson. They were part of a tough group of soldiers called 'housecarls', who were famous for splitting the skulls of their enemies with huge axes. His other rival, Harald Hardrada, also had some frightening soldiers. The best Norwegian soldiers were called 'berserkers', because they were famous for going crazy or 'berserk' when fighting.

English housecarls. The front soldier holds a deadly battle-axe.

William's 2nd problem: He had no English friends.

Harold Godwinson was supported by most people in England, including two powerful groups – the nobles and the leaders of the Church. This picture shows English nobles offering Harold Godwinson a crown. (Can you see that the men have huge battle-axes, which were used by the English?)

In contrast, William had never been to England and had very few friends there. William organised an army of about 6000 knights to attack England. This was quite a small army and they were greatly outnumbered by over 2 million English people.

The English nobles wanted Harold to be the next king. This shows them offering him the crown.

William's 3rd problem: Crossing the English Channel with an army was very dangerous

Before William could become king he would have to take the Norman army across the English Channel in tiny boats. The Normans had no boats and needed to build a huge fleet in just a few weeks. William had never taken an army to another country by sea. This was much more dangerous than it is today. The boats of the time were very small and could only take a few men or horses. There was a good chance of a storm. In a bad storm the little boats would sink. Many of the Normans were frightened about going to sea.

Was William lucky and clever?

Things can go well when you are lucky or when you make some clever decisions. Very successful people are often clever but sometimes need a bit of luck too. Let's compare what Harold Godwinson and William did in 1066 as they got ready for battle. You must work out which one was luckier and more clever by looking at the story.

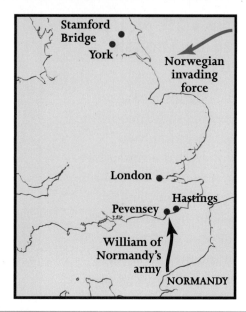

Stage 1

What Harold did

In the summer of 1066, Harold Godwinson organised a huge army and a massive fleet of 700 ships to stop William invading. In August, the soldiers and sailors said that they had to go back to their homes to help with the harvest. On 8 September Godwinson sent the soldiers and sailors home.

What William did

By July, William was ready to attack. Most people thought he would attack immediately. Instead William waited and waited. He knew that most of the English soldiers and sailors would need to go home before the summer was over to help with the harvest.

Stage 2

What Harold did next

Just after Harold Godwinson sent his soldiers home, Hardrada and his Norwegian army landed in Yorkshire. Harold marched north to fight him. As he travelled towards York he quickly gathered a new army. After a rapid march, his army reached Stamford Bridge where the Norwegians were based. They slaughtered the Norwegian army and Hardrada was killed.

What William did next

During most of September William couldn't sail across the English Channel, because the wind was blowing in the wrong direction. On 27 September, the wind changed. William and his army, the Normans, crossed safely. With Harold Godwinson busy in Yorkshire no one tried to stop his army when they landed. Meanwhile Hardrada, one of his two enemies, was killed by Harold without William having to lift a finger.

1 Look at Stages 1 and 2 and decide who was more clever.

What should Harold do now?

Harold Godwinson and his men were exhausted after their great victory against Hardrada at Stamford Bridge, but they had little chance to rest. Four or five days after the battle, Harold heard that William had landed on the south coast of England, near Hastings. Harold returned quickly to London. What should he do next? This would decide whether he would live or die.

Should he march out from London and fight William?   **OR**   **Should he play a waiting game and avoid a battle with William?**

His advisers gave him different pieces of advice:

A 'We have heard reports that the Normans are riding round the countryside near Hastings burning villages and stealing anything valuable. Unless they are stopped they will do great damage.'

D 'The battle plan at Stamford Bridge worked brilliantly. By immediately attacking the enemy we took them by surprise and destroyed them.'

B 'It will soon be winter. The Normans will find it difficult to find food. Their great war-horses will starve.'

E 'We smashed the army of Harald Hardrada, the greatest Viking of the age. This shows that God is on our side and will give us more victories.'

C 'Our men are very tired. They have marched to Yorkshire and back. They fought a gruelling battle and now they are exhausted.'

F 'The soldiers are excited by how well they did at Stamford Bridge. They are full of confidence and ready to take on anyone.'

2 Look at each of the pieces of advice and decide whether it is a reason to fight or a reason to wait.

3 What would your advice be to Harold. Should he march or should he wait?

My advice to Harold would be _____

Because _____

Hastings: Battle to the death

Harold decided to march to Hastings and fight William. The two sides met on Saturday 14 October 1066, near Hastings. We're going to take an in-depth look at two different sources in order to piece together what happened at the Battle of Hastings. One was written a few years after the battle by a monk called William of Malmesbury. The other source is the famous Bayeux Tapestry.

The start of the fighting

The English passed the night without sleep, in drinking and singing, and in the morning marched quickly to battle. The Normans passed the whole night in prayer and held a church service in the morning.

*The English were all on foot, armed with battle-axes. They protected themselves by joining their shields together, and this made them into a very strong force. The Normans had foot-soldiers and **cavalry** (soldiers on horse-back). Their foot-soldiers stood in the front armed with bows and arrows, while their cavalry was at the back.*

William of Malmesbury

The Bayeux Tapestry shows the start of the battle.
The English foot-soldiers carry axes and battle with the Norman knights on horseback.

What did William do during the battle?

Before the fighting started William looked confident and calm. He spoke to his troops, telling them that they would win because God was on their side.

When the fighting began, William shouted to his soldiers to encourage them. He was the first to rush forward to attack. He fought in the middle of the enemy. He seemed to be everywhere, fierce and furious. Three of his horses were killed under him. This did not frighten him. His bodyguard urged him to be careful, but he still continued to fight. No doubt the hand of God protected him, though the enemy aimed many spears at him.

William of Malmesbury

Detail of stitching from the Bayeux Tapestry

William lifts his helmet to show his men that he is still alive and will lead them to victory. This makes his men brave.

Fierce fighting and clever plans

For many hours there was fierce fighting and neither side gave way. Many were killed on both sides. Then William thought of a good battle plan – he ordered his troops to **pretend to run away**. *The solid wall of the English fell apart as they chased the fleeing Normans. The Normans turned around and attacked the English. This trick led to the death of many English but it did not end the battle. The English regrouped on the hillside and killed the Normans as they struggled up the hill.*

What did Harold do during the battle?

The battle went on for hours, with first one side and then the other doing better. The English were ready to carry on fighting as long as Harold lived. He was very brave. Not content to be a general, he fought like an ordinary soldier. He killed many of the enemy at close quarters. Sometimes he killed a soldier and horse with a single blow. The Normans were afraid to approach him.

William of Malmesbury

The two armies fought fiercely and many men were killed on both sides. Here Norman horses stumble as they attack the English.

16

How did the battle end?

The battle continued as long as Harold was alive. He was able to stop the English from giving up. The Normans were not able to kill him in hand-to-hand fighting. It was only a long-range arrow that brought him down. The arrow pierced his brain and Harold was killed. One of the Norman soldiers hacked at his legs as he lay on the ground. The English soldiers then gave up fighting and ran. The Normans chased after them until night fell. William and the Norman soldiers had won.

William of Malmesbury

Harold is killed by a Norman archer. The arrow has gone through his eye into his brain. In the bottom of the picture the English dead are robbed of their weapons and armour.

1 Describe what happened at the battle in your own words using information from both sources.

What happened during the battle? _____

What did William do? _____

What did Harold do? _____

Why did William win? _____

What mistakes did Harold make? _____

2 *A source is useful to you if it gives you lots of the information you need. Were the pictures or the writing more useful to you in helping you to answer question 1?*

Interpreting the Battle of Hastings

A modern artist called Angus MacBride has tried to give us an idea of what the Battle of Hastings was like by painting a scene from the battle. He used different sources to make sure his painting was accurate. He also used his imagination. Let's take a look at the way he worked.

Source 1

The English fought back bravely, throwing spears, axes and stones. The Normans were about to retreat when William pushed himself to the front and said, 'Look at me! I am still alive, and with God's help, I shall be the winner!' With these words he made the Normans brave again.

William of Poitiers.

Source 1 is a written account of the battle by a Norman called William of Poitiers. He describes how William of Normandy urges on his soldiers as they are starting to flee. With their leader ahead, the Normans continue their fight against the English.

Source 2

This is a scene from the Bayeux tapestry. You can see William raising his helmet to let his army know that he is still alive. The Normans fight on bravely.

1 Make a list of how many similarities you can see between the story that is shown in sources 1 and 2 and in the modern painting (source 3).

2 Make a list of any differences between the story in the modern painting and in the other two sources.

Source 3

This is a modern painting of the Battle of Hastings by Angus MacBride. He has drawn the battle based on what he knows about it from the sources and his imagination.

After his great victory at the Battle of Hastings, William became King of England. He was given the nickname William the Conqueror. But he still faced one big problem. The English had wanted Harold to become king. Nobody liked William and the Norman army. William was afraid that the English might gather their own army and attack him.

> I've conquered England but I don't feel safe. The English hate us Normans. They will kill us all if they get the chance. What I need is a strong army.

William's Solution: Stage 1

The new king needed a larger army to support him. At that time, gifts of land were given to the most powerful men, and in return, they had to supply knights for the king's army. This system of land for knights is called **feudalism**. Each gift of land was known as a **feudum**.

William decided to give much of the land of England to a small number of his Norman friends. These powerful Normans were called barons. In return for land in England, the barons each promised to give William about 30 knights for his army. The land the barons were given was made up of lots of villages. The barons gave a village to each knight who promised to fight for William when he was needed.

There were nearly 200 barons. If each one gave the king 30 knights, this made an army of 6,000 knights.

> Good. Feudalism has given me an army of 6,000 knights. Now I feel a lot safer.

Armed Norman knights ride out to fight. The feudal system gave William an army of men like this.

William's Solution: Stage 2

Wait a minute. I'm glad I've got an army of 6,000 tough Norman knights but there are two million English people. How can 6,000 control two million? What can I do?

William's knights needed to have a base in every part of the country so that they could control the ordinary people. To provide the knights with a base William told his barons to build castles. William also built some of his own castles. Although this may seem obvious to us now, castles were quite new at the time.

Norman castles are often called 'motte and bailey' castles because they were built in two parts. There was a large yard called a 'bailey' where the knights could keep their horses and servants. This was surrounded by a tall wooden fence. There was also a high mound of earth called a 'motte', with a wooden tower on top. The knights lived inside the motte, and could stay there when they were being attacked. Even if a large number of English people decided to attack the castle, a small group of Normans could defend a motte while they waited for help.

The Norman knights helped the baron who ruled over that area of the country. In the daytime they collected money and food from the English. At night they could return to the safety of their castles and sleep.

You Decide

1 You are one of the followers of Hereward the Wake. He was an English man who refused to accept the Normans as rulers of England and he fought against them. Hereward has sent you as a spy to find out what the Normans are doing. Write a report for Hereward describing how William used feudalism and castles to help him in his fight against the English.

Norman knights near one of their motte and bailey castles. One knight is wounded but he can be taken to safety in the castle.

... They'll kill us if they get a chance

> The English still refuse to accept me as king. I will have to do something more drastic.

Further problems: Stage 3

It was 1069, three years after the Battle of Hastings, and many of the English still refused to obey William. The people of the north and the east of England caused him the most trouble. In January, he sent one of his friends, Robert Commines, to take charge of the north. When Robert reached Durham, he was attacked on the street by local people. He ran to the bishop's house to get help. The mob followed and burned him to death inside the bishop's house.

A few months later William's problems got worse. A huge Danish war fleet appeared and attacked the east coast. The Danes landed in Yorkshire. The local English people rose up and joined forces with the Danes. In September the city of York was captured and the Norman soldiers in the city were killed.

The Normans burnt down villages to force the English to surrender. Here a woman and child flee as their house is burnt.

> 2 The Harrying of the North was one of the most brutal events in the whole of English history. Twenty years later many villages remained empty and in ruins. Explain why you think William ordered his men to carry out this brutal act.

The Harrying of the North

William and the Norman army slowly marched across the north of England towards York. They killed all the Englishmen they met and set fire to every village they passed through. As a result, thousands of ordinary people lost the food they were growing and storing and starved to death. By December of 1069, he reached and recaptured York.

William's brutal march through the north of England became known as the Harrying of the North.

The Danish army moved south to Lincolnshire and linked up with the English rebel leader, Hereward the Wake. In 1070, William offered the Danes a bribe and they agreed to leave England. William marched into Lincolnshire and the English rebels ran away. Hereward escaped and was never captured.

William's success

At the beginning of this book we talked about how some kings were successful and others were unsuccessful. As we have seen, William was very successful. He was a strong, powerful king. He was successful because he was very clever and tough on his enemies.

1 People at the time disagreed about why William was so successful. Here are two statements. One was written by an English man and one by a Norman man. Can you work out which one is which?

> *The king was one of the cleverest and greatest of all kings. Nothing was ever too difficult or dangerous for him.*

> *He was hard on poor men. He was very strict and took much gold and silver from the poor. He loved greediness above all.*

2 Look back through the work you have done on William. What parts of the story show you that William was clever?

3 What parts of the story tell you that William was cruel?

4 Is it possible that both the statements in Question 1 are right? Explain your answer.

You Decide

5 You are an English monk living in 1086. William has just died. Write a short **biography** of William (a biography tells the story of his life). Make it obvious from the way you tell the story that you did not like him and you think he was cruel.

When William the Conqueror died the future seemed clear. He left Normandy to his oldest son, Robert. He gave England to his next son, William Rufus. His third son, Henry, got nothing. A few years later William Rufus was dead and Robert was in prison for life. Henry was King of England and Duke of Normandy. How did this happen? One historian thinks that Henry arranged the murder of his brother so he could become king.

William Rufus, you have the crown of England. Robert will have Normandy. But for you Henry, nothing.

So, who killed William Rufus?

Writers at the time said that William Rufus was killed in a hunting accident while he was riding through the woods in 1100. A modern historian, Christopher Brooke, is not so sure. He suspects the youngest brother, Henry, of murder. Look at the information that follows and see if you think Henry ordered the killing of William Rufus.

You Decide

1 You are investigating the charge that Henry ordered the killing of his brother, William Rufus. As you look at each of the following pieces of information decide whether it fits with the theory that Henry ordered the murder.

On 2 August 1100, William Rufus went out hunting in the New Forest, near Winchester. His younger brother, Henry, was one of the hunting party. While they were hunting, Rufus and a knight called Walter Tirel got separated from the others. While the two men were alone, Rufus was killed by an arrow from Tirel's bow. Afterwards Henry said it was an accident. Tirel did not wait to explain what had happened. He immediately fled from the Forest and left the country.

Henry's background

While we don't know what exactly happened to Rufus, we do know that Henry was very violent. As a young man he lost his temper at the castle in Rouen and threw a local man over the battlements. Later, during a family argument, he gave permission for two of his own granddaughters to be blinded. When Henry became king we know that he arrested his older brother, Robert, and kept him in prison for over thirty years until he died.

the death of Rufus

What Henry did after the killing

Henry did not chase after Tirel and did not order anyone else to chase him. Tirel made his way to the coast and was able to leave the country. Henry's first thought was not to arrange a funeral for his brother. He immediately raced to the city of Winchester where Rufus had all his treasure. Henry grabbed the treasure and then rode at tremendous speed to London. Three days later he was crowned king. Afterwards he did nothing to track down Tirel and no one was ever punished for the killing. Henry treated Tirel's family well and promoted many of them to good jobs.

The older brother

After Rufus's death, Henry's other brother Robert could also have declared himself king. But, at that time, Robert was thousands of miles away fighting in the crusades. Henry knew that Robert was travelling slowly back home and could do nothing. Henry was in England and was able to seize the crown immediately. If William Rufus had died after Robert's return it would have been more difficult for Henry to take over as king.

William Rufus was hunting in the forest when he was killed. Do you think his death was an accident?

---

2 Do you think that Henry ordered the killing of his brother, William Rufus? In your answer you should include:

The case: The death of William Rufus

Did Henry have a motive?

_____

What kind of character was Henry?

_____

Do any of the **events** fit in with the theory that Henry was guilty of murder?

_____

Matilda's bid for power

Most kings wanted one of their family to carry on as ruler after their death. Henry I planned that his son, William, should be the next king. In 1120, young William was killed in a shipwreck while crossing the English Channel. With William gone, who could take over? Henry shocked and astonished his barons by announcing that his daughter, Matilda, would be the next ruler of England.

Matilda at the time of her first marriage. Did men at the time think that women like Matilda should have power?

Why were the barons so shocked at the idea of a woman ruling England? See if you can work this out from the following three sources. These sources are comments about women, written by men at the time.

'The Church says women should be subject to men. It is natural for women to serve men and children to serve their parents. This is because the lesser people should serve the greater people. Women must be silent in church as it says in the Bible. Saint Paul says that women must not teach or have authority over men.'

'There are two kinds of dogs: well trained dogs are silent and do as they are told, badly trained dogs are bad tempered and fond of barking. So it is with women. The best are silent and do what men say. The worst are loud and troublesome.'

'The law says that married women are like children. Anything a married woman has is the property of her husband. Just as a father has a right to beat his children to make them behave, a husband has the right to beat his wife if she does not behave properly.'

So what happened to Matilda?

Henry I made the barons promise to obey Matilda as their next ruler. They were very frightened of Henry so they agreed. Secretly many were unhappy about the idea of a woman ruler. Matilda's cousin, Stephen, plotted to take over instead. As soon as the old king died, the barons said they did not want a woman ruler and Stephen became king.

Was Matilda a good leader?

Historians agree that Matilda had a big problem: the men of the time were very sexist. For ten years Matilda tried to take back power in England from her cousin, Stephen. In the end, Matilda admitted defeat and went to live in Normandy. But what was she like as a leader? Historians have very different views of her as a leader:

View 1:
Matilda was not a good leader. She made some serious mistakes.

View 2:
Matilda was a good leader. She had many of the skills needed to rule a country.

Matilda's fight for power

A At first, Matilda refused to accept defeat. She declared war on Stephen. She arrived from France with a small army. Fighting began. Although he had a much bigger army, Stephen was unable to defeat Matilda. In 1141, Matilda's army won a major battle at Lincoln and Stephen was captured.

B With Stephen a prisoner, Matilda got ready to be crowned in London. The people of London disliked her because she was very proud. She announced that the Londoners must pay new taxes. The Londoners attacked her and chased her out of the city, so she was not crowned as queen. Later Stephen was freed in a swap for another prisoner.

C Matilda was always close to the action and she was very brave. At Christmas 1142, Stephen and his army trapped her inside Oxford Castle. It seemed certain that she would be captured. To everyone's amazement she climbed down the walls of the castle at night. Then, wearing white to camouflage herself against the snow, she crossed the frozen River Thames on foot and escaped. She fled to Normandy where she lived for the rest of her life.

1 Look at the information in the box on Matilda's fight for power. Decide whether each piece of information supports View 1 or View 2.

2 Do you think Matilda was a good leader?

A licence to kill? The death of Becket

In the James Bond stories the hero has 'a licence to kill' his enemies. This means that the government has given him permission to murder. Did the knights in this story also have a licence to kill? Henry II was the king at that time. Had he given them permission to murder?

It was Tuesday, 29 December 1170. The time was 4.30 in the afternoon. The place was Canterbury Cathedral, where Thomas Becket was archbishop. Something happened there that amazed and horrified people throughout Europe. **Becket was hacked to death in his own cathedral! The killers sliced off the top of his head and scattered blood and brains across the cathedral floor.** His killers were four knights who worked for the king, Henry II. People immediately blamed Henry for the killing and called him a murderer. The King of France said that Henry was guilty of one of the worst crimes in history. But was he?

Some of the basic facts are clear.

◆ Henry II was in France. The knights had been with him and set off for England on the evening of Christmas Day, four days before the killing.

◆ The knights arrived in Canterbury on the morning of 29 December. They had an angry meeting with Thomas in the early afternoon.

◆ They argued about the way Thomas was treating bishops who were friends of Henry. Thomas had **suspended** the bishops (refused to let them work) because they had helped Henry in a major church service without permission from Thomas.

◆ The knights left the first meeting in a very bad mood. A little while later they returned for the final meeting. When they returned they were carrying weapons.

Notice that Henry II was not there. He was in France at the time. To prove that the knights had a 'licence to kill' you must show that Henry sent the knights to Canterbury with instructions to kill Thomas. If Henry gave permission for the killing then he is responsible for murder!

The walls of Canterbury. Becket let the knights enter the city. Do you think he wanted to die?

One knight points his finger and shouts. Why were the knights so angry?

Only one man witnessed the final moments. He was a priest called Edward Grim.

The leader of the killers was a knight called Reginald. His special sign was a bear. Can you see the bear on his shield?

Becket's head is sliced open as he kneels before the altar. Why do you think Becket waited in this particular place?

29

... The death of Becket

There were witnesses who can tell us about the killing. Becket was not alone in Canterbury Cathedral when he was killed. Edward Grim (a priest) and Gervase (a monk) both saw the knights return for the second meeting with Thomas. You ask them some questions to find out what they saw.

Witness 1: Edward Grim

Edward Grim was a priest. He was visiting the cathedral at the time of the killing. He was injured during the murder.

Question 1: Tell me what happened when the knights came back to the cathedral for the second time.

'The monks wanted to lock the doors to stop the knights getting in. Thomas ordered that the doors should be opened. When the knights entered the cathedral Thomas did not run from them.'

Question 2: Did the knights say anything to Becket?

'They demanded that he should stop punishing those bishops who were friends of the king, and allow them to go back to work. Thomas refused. They threatened to kill him. Thomas replied that he was ready to die so that the Church would be free.'

Question 3: Do you think the knights planned to kill him at this stage?

'They tried to drag him out of the cathedral but Thomas held on to a pillar. It was not clear whether they wanted to kill him outside the cathedral or if they wanted to take him out as a prisoner.'

Question 4: Did you see who struck the first blow?

'Thomas clearly knew one of the knights, one called Reginald. He pushed Reginald away and called him a disloyal fool. Reginald went into a terrible rage at this and raised his sword. Reginald said that he was loyal to the king. Thomas then went to pray and Reginald struck him on the head.'

Question 5: What happened next?

'My arm was also cut with the first blow that hit Thomas. I was trying to protect the archbishop while all the other monks and priests ran for safety. Thomas was struck two more times and he fell. Another knight sliced off the top of the archbishop's head. White brains and red blood spilled out.'

Question 6: Did anyone else join in the violence?

'A clergyman called Hugh, who was with the knights, placed his foot on Becket's neck and scattered the brains across the floor, shouting to the rest, 'Let us go, knights, he will not be getting up again.'

Witness 2: Gervase of Canterbury

Gervase was a monk at Canterbury. He knew Thomas well. He ran away with the other Canterbury monks during the final attack on Thomas.

Question 1: Right, Gervase, can you tell me who the killers were?

'They were the king's men: Reginald Fitzurse, Hugh de Morville, William de Tracey, and Richard Brito.'

Question 2: Did Thomas have a chance to escape before the second meeting?

'The archbishop's friends urged him tearfully to escape. He refused, and slowly prepared for the evening service in the cathedral. It seemed that he was getting ready to die. He ordered that the door of the cathedral should be kept open. While he was speaking the killers rushed in.'

Question 3: Did the knights have any weapons?

'They wore armour under their clothes. Three of them carried hatchets in their left bands, and one a two-headed axe, while all of them brandished drawn swords in their right hands.'

Question 4: What did the knights do once in the cathedral?

'As they entered the open door of the cathedral they divided up. Reginald Fitzurse turned to the left, while the three others went right. Fitzurse was the first to find the archbishop. Thomas said, "Here I am, Reginald. I have been kind to you before now. Yet you come to me with weapons in your hands."'

Question 5: You ran away at this point so you didn't actually see the killing. Were there any clues that they were instructed to kill Thomas by Henry II?

'After the murder they ran through the cathedral. They shouted out, "We are knights of the king! Out of our way; he is dead!"'

---

1 Using information from both witnesses, write the first part of your report about the murder. This will help you decide whether Henry was guilty of murder. Make sure your report covers the following points:

◆ What happened (summarise the story in your own words).

◆ Did the knights plan to kill Thomas?

◆ Could Becket have escaped if he wanted to?

◆ Is there any evidence that the knights were carrying out the orders of Henry II?

31

Henry and Becket: a deadly quarrel?

Before you come to a final decision about whether Henry was guilty of murder you need to know more about the relationship between Henry and Becket. Did they get on? At first Henry seemed to like Becket but what made him change his mind? Was this a motive for murder? Did Henry encourage the knights to kill Becket? Read the following factfiles and decide whether Henry was guilty or innocent of murder.

Henry II and Becket often argued about religious matters. Kings and their archbishops often disagreed about who should have most power.

File 1:

Becket becomes Archbishop of Canterbury

Many kings of England argued with Church leaders. Both kings and archbishops thought it was their job to be in charge and tell people what to do. They often didn't agree. William the Conqueror and William Rufus, for example, argued fiercely with church leaders. Henry II actually chose Becket to be his archbishop because he wanted someone that he would get on well with.

Thomas Becket and Henry had been very close friends. Thomas's family were merchants in London. When Henry became king in 1154, he gave Thomas a top government job as his chancellor. As a result, Thomas became rich. He enjoyed working for the king and lived a life of luxury.

In 1162 Henry decided that Thomas should be the new Archbishop of Canterbury. This was a surprise to most people because Thomas was not a priest and was not even religious. King Henry expected that Thomas would be very grateful to him for giving him such an important job in the Church.

File 2:
A personality change

Once he was archbishop, Thomas's personality changed. He became very serious and interested in religion. He started arguing with the king. They disagreed about how clergymen should be treated if they broke the law. The king wanted to punish them in his own royal courts. Thomas said that clergymen should be punished by special church courts which gave out softer penalties. Henry was amazed. Thomas owed him everything but showed no gratitude. The arguments got worse and worse. After two years, Thomas fled the country and went into exile in France.

File 3:
Astonished and angry

Thomas spent six years out of the country. In July 1170, Thomas and Henry met and agreed to end their quarrel. Thomas returned to England on 1 December. Soon afterwards, as we know, he suspended a number of bishops who were Henry's friends. The bishops went to see the king to complain. Henry was astonished and very angry.

File 4:
A fateful speech

Henry asked his barons and knights how Becket should be punished. Some said that Becket should be arrested; others said that he should be killed. On Christmas Day Henry made a fateful speech. It is difficult to be sure exactly what he said. One version is that he said:

'Will no one get rid of this troublesome priest for me?'

Another version is that he said:

'You are lazy traitors for letting me be so badly treated by this low-born priest.'

The four knights who carried out the killing heard Henry's speech and made a secret plan to travel to Canterbury. There is no evidence that they spoke to the king about their plans. Four days later they killed Thomas Becket.

---

1 *Write the second part of your report using all the evidence you have read. To make a final decision on whether Henry II was guilty of murder you need to consider the following points.*
   ◆ *Did Henry want to kill Becket?*
   ◆ *Did Henry tell the knights to kill Becket?*
   ◆ *Did the knights set out to kill Becket?*
   ◆ *Did Becket want to die?*

Royal justice

In Bury Saint Edmunds, in Suffolk, eight men broke into the huge church in the centre of the town. They planned to rob some of the valuable treasure they knew was kept there. The plan went badly wrong and they were caught. So, what happened next?

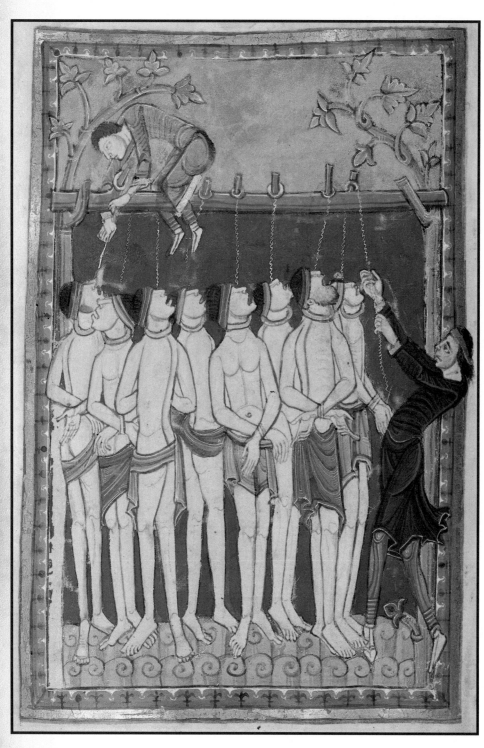

The abbot of Bury was in charge of the local abbey. He was a rich landowner and had the power of life and death over local criminals. In the early Middle Ages all barons and landowners had their own courts. He decided to *execute* (put to death) the robbers by hanging them.

The execution took place out in the open so that everybody could see. The abbot made sure it was carried out properly. The robbers were tied up and stripped almost naked. They were blindfolded and then hanged. Assistants tugged hard on the chains round their necks to make sure they were dead. Afterwards the bodies were left there as a warning to everybody not to steal.

Henry II and changes to the courts

The system of courts changed in the 12th Century. Henry II wanted to strengthen the power of the monarchy. He did this in different ways. One way was to change the court system. He wanted to take power away from the local lords and landowners (people like the abbot of Bury).

Henry ordered that serious crimes should be dealt with in the royal courts and not in the courts of other lords. Only the royal courts could execute people. If prisoners were found guilty and put to death, all their goods were seized and kept for the king. As a result the king made a lot of money.

Were the royal courts any fairer?

Royal judges toured England and regularly visited the whole country. In each county, local criminals were kept in the king's castle until the judges arrived. The royal judges relied on juries to help them decide on each case. Each jury consisted of twelve respectable local men who were supposed to know the criminals and the case. They told the king's judge whether or not they thought the accused were guilty.

The king's courts also dealt with arguments about land. This made lots of money for the king too. If it was just an argument and not a serious crime, people had to pay the courts to get the judges to hear their concerns.

These prisoners are waiting for their trial. Can you see that they are chained together to stop them from escaping?

1 *How did the court system change during the reign of Henry II?*

2 *Why do you think Henry changed the court system?*

The mystery of the kind-hearted jury

The judges of the royal courts travelled around the country hearing cases against criminals. They depended on local men to make up the juries and give them advice. Kings liked the royal courts because they made lots of money for them. Kings were particularly happy if lots of people were found guilty. This was because most guilty prisoners were hanged and the king took all their money and goods.

Let's look at some real court cases from medieval times. All the records that follow come from Salisbury court in September 1303. Do you notice anything surprising about these cases?

Edward de Marlborough for burgling the house of John of Opeshul. Pleads not guilty. Jury says not guilty. So he is freed.

Roger Street and William Altheworld for burgling the house of Margery la Rayne. Plead not guilty. Jury says not guilty. So they are freed.

Criminals were usually put to death if they were found guilty.

Walter Church for receiving stolen goods. Pleads not guilty. Jury says not guilty. So he is freed.

John Warrener for stealing a chalice. Pleads not guilty. Jury says not guilty. So he is freed.

One historian called Barbara Hanawalt has looked very closely at the way juries worked. She has made a very surprising discovery.

I looked at court cases for eight counties over a long period of time 1300–1348. Only a quarter of all the people on trial were found guilty. The juries said that the great majority were not guilty.

This is very mysterious. It seems that many criminals got away with their crimes because the jury did not want to find them guilty.

You Decide

1 You are a local person on the jury of a royal court. A woman from your village has been caught stealing from the lord's house. You must decide what advice to give the judge. Look at the facts below. Make a table with the facts on one side and your thoughts on the other. Would you find the woman guilty?

- ◆ All people found guilty were hanged if they were twelve or older, and if they stole goods worth 12 pence or more.

- ◆ Before their trial prisoners were kept for months in prison in the local castle. Conditions in these prisons were terrible.

- ◆ Juries were made up of local people. The men on the jury usually knew the prisoners and knew their families.

- ◆ The years 1300–1348 included times of famine when ordinary people had no food. Many criminals stole because they were starving.

A woman stealing. Why did many criminals like this escape punishment?

A king's army: cavalry and infantry

A medieval king was above all else a warrior – a fighting man. To be successful he needed a good army. Most armies had two sections: the cavalry were made up of rich knights on horseback. They rode into battle. The infantry was made up of poor foot-soldiers, archers and cross-bow men. They went into battle on foot because they couldn't afford expensive war-horses. But who was more important?

Sieges of castles were much more common than battles. During a siege, an enemy army surrounds a castle and tries to take it over. Look at the siege of Rochester Castle and see which part of the army was more important during the siege: the **cavalry** or the **infantry**.

Rich knights looked down at poor infantry like this but were the cavalry really more important?

Look at this account of a siege to work out who was more important: cavalry or infantry.

The Siege of Rochester in 1215

Heavy casualties

In 1215, towards the end of the reign of King John, there was a war between John and some of his barons. The barons seized the royal castle at Rochester. John was very angry and besieged them. The castle was very strong and the siege lasted two months. John and his knights could do little to get the barons out of the castle. Skilled cross-bow men inside the castle shot at anyone they saw outside. Many of John's army were killed in this way.

Let's eat the horses!

The barons and their army inside the castle could not go outside without being killed by John's army. They began to run out of food and supplies and began to starve to death. The knights from the barons' army inside the castle could make no use of their expensive war-horses so they killed them and ate them.

Cut off their hands and feet!

John got frustrated that the barons refused to surrender. He ordered some daring foot-soldiers from his infantry to go to the castle walls. Under a deadly rain of cross-bow fire from the castle, they made fires at the bottom of the walls and hacked away at the stone. Eventually the walls began to collapse. The barons still refused to surrender. They ordered their injured men to leave the castle to save food for those who remained. As these men came outside they were captured by John's army and punished by having their hands and feet cut off.

Hang all the cross-bow men!

Finally, the rest of the barons and their army were forced to surrender. John wanted to kill them all. He later changed his mind and let them live, with one exception: he ordered that all the cross-bow men should be hanged because they had already killed so many of his own men.

---

1 Look back at the story. What evidence can you find that knights on horses were not very important during the siege?

2 How many examples can you find of foot-soldiers playing an important part in the siege?

3 Overall, who was more important at the siege of Rochester: **cavalry** or **infantry**? Why do you think this?

John and the barons

The siege of Rochester took place at the end of King John's reign. We know from this that the barons were not happy with the way that John ruled the country. He was not very popular. But what did he do to make himself so disliked?

Kings relied on their barons and church leaders for support. The barons and priests expected their kings to act in a particular way. They thought that good kings should:

◆ Be great warriors. They should fight and defeat their enemies and protect the country.

◆ Get on well with their nobility. They should give them interesting jobs and treat them with respect.

◆ Support the Church. They should fight against enemies of the Church.

> 1 Read the files about John and how he ruled as king. Make a list of things that made him unpopular with the barons and church leaders.

King John hunting.
Why was he so unpopular?

File 1:
John's prisoners

In 1194, before he became king, he shocked the world by beheading some French knights that he had captured in war. Noble prisoners-of-war were not usually treated in this way. Captured knights were usually released once their relatives had paid a ransom.

A few years later he had an argument with a great noble called William de Braose. John captured William's wife, Matilda, and starved her to death in a dungeon at Windsor Castle.

File 2:
Don't call me Soft-Sword!

Medieval warriors practised for war by taking part in tournaments. Unlike many other kings, John does not seem to have been very interested in tournaments. One of his nicknames as a young man was 'Soft-Sword' because he was not very good at fighting. Despite this, John spent much of his reign fighting a war against the French. He was very unsuccessful in this war. In 1204, the French conquered Normandy. John spent the following ten years trying to win Normandy back, but without success.

File 3:
Top jobs for foreigners

John did not trust his barons and nobles in England. He gave the top jobs to foreigners, as he trusted them more. He also wanted to make sure that the barons obeyed him. He tried to do this by making them frightened of him. This did not work. The barons just became angry.

File 4:
The Church goes on strike

John was not very religious, so he gave very little money to the Church. He often argued with church leaders. In 1205, John and his archbishop of Canterbury, had a big argument with the Pope (the head of the Catholic Church). They argued about who should be the next archbishop.

This disagreement went on for years and made the church leaders very angry. In 1208, the Pope ordered all priests in the Church in England to go on strike and stop all church services. For five years the churches were closed. In the end John had to give in and admit he was wrong.

File 5:
Chaos and war

John's reign ended in chaos. He made another attempt to recapture Normandy in 1214. Many barons refused to help him. His armies in France were defeated yet again.

In 1215, a war began between John and his barons. (The siege of Rochester was part of this war.) The barons thought that John taxed them too heavily to pay for his war with France and interfered with their affairs.

The barons took control of London and forced John to sign a charter agreeing to many of their demands. This document is known as Magna Carta (meaning the Great Charter).

The signing of the Magna Carta did not end the conflict because John didn't keep his side of the bargain. A French army then invaded England to support the barons. John died in 1216, leaving the barons in a position of power.

Magna Carta

The signing of Magna Carta is seen as a great moment in the history of Britain. The Magna Carta was an agreement, between King John and the barons, that gave ordinary people rights. But did the Magna Carta really give the ordinary people what they wanted? Some people think that the Magna Carta was just a list of complaints made by the barons, which did not help the ordinary people. Below are some of the main points.

When a baron dies there should be a limit on the money his family has to pay to the king.

So, do we all agree?

There should be no extra taxes unless barons meet and agree to the new tax.

No one should be fined heavily by the king's judges for minor crimes. No one should be imprisoned without a fair trial.

Merchants should be allowed to trade without interference from the government.

The king's judges should be fair to everyone and should not take bribes.

Anyone can leave or enter the country, unless they have committed a crime or a war is on.

A council of 25 barons should help the king to rule the country.

---

1 Look at each of the points from Magna Carta. Copy the following table and write out each point in the correct column.

Points to do with the rights of ordinary people	Points to do with the selfish interests of the barons

Imagine that the government has asked you to produce a Modern Magna Carta. They want it to be an official list of human rights. If you had to include one point from the original Magna Carta, which one would it be? Can you think of some other human rights that are important today and should go into the Modern Magna Carta?

England and the Celtic lands

People today disagree about whether the English government should have any power over the other parts of the British Isles. This argument began back in the Middle Ages. The kings of England thought it was part of their mission to conquer and control all of the British Isles. They tried to take over Wales, Ireland and Scotland. Your job in this unit is to work out how far the kings of England were successful in their mission.

The English kings V the Irish

1169–1171: English barons invaded and conquered much of Ireland. Henry II declared himself 'Lord of Ireland' and he visited the country to show that he was in charge.

1200–1300: The English built castles all across Ireland. English-style government, law and language was forced on the Irish.

1400–1500: English control in most of Ireland collapsed. The English government still ruled over a very small area around Dublin. Outside this area the Irish were free from English rule.

An English-Norman knight rides down an Irish warrior.

The English kings V the Scots

1140–1157: During a civil war in England the king of Scotland conquered the most northerly parts of England, including important castles at Carlisle and Newcastle.

1290–1305: The last member of the royal family of Scotland died. Edward I of England took control. A Scots army led by William Wallace fought against him. Wallace was defeated and executed.

1306–1314: A new Scots king called Robert Bruce fought successfully against the English. An English army was destroyed at the Battle of Bannockburn. Afterwards Scotland was free from English rule.

The English kings V the Welsh

1090–1120: The English conquered much of the rich, low-lying land of south Wales.

1276–1283: Edward I fought against the Welsh of north Wales. Llywelyn, the Welsh prince who ruled this area, was killed in 1282. Afterwards Edward built a series of castles so that the Welsh couldn't be free.

1400–1406: The Welsh people rebelled against English rule. They were led by Owain Glyndwr. He was defeated in 1406. English rule over Wales continued.

1 For each country – Ireland, Scotland and Wales – write a brief paragraph saying whether the English kings were:
   - ◆ completely successful
   - ◆ partly successful
   - ◆ completely unsuccessful

   Write it in your own words and give examples to support what you say.

2 Do you think that, **overall**, the English kings were successful in their attempt to control the other people of the British Isles?

The Welsh prince, Llywelyn was beheaded by the English at the Tower of London.

45

The changing face of the royal castle

Edward I became king in 1272 and spent most of his money on building castles in Wales. Edward's castles were very different from the ones built by the Normans in 1066. In the 200 years between, people had learnt how to build better and stronger castles.

It is your job to find out how different Edward's castles were to any that had been built before. Take a look at the pictures of the Norman castle and Edward's castle. Can you see how much they have changed?

Wooden central tower or keep — the strongest point in the castle.

Earth mound known as a motte.

Defended outer section called a bailey.

Wooden wall with no towers.

An early Norman castle made of motte and bailey.
These castles were not very strong.

---

1 Finish the sentences which describe some of the differences between the two types of castle.

The building materials for the early Norman castles were timber and earth.
By contrast, Edward's castles were made of _____

The strongest part of the Norman castles was a mound of earth at the centre of the castle called a motte. By contrast, the strongest part of Edward's castles was _____

Early Norman castles could be built very quickly. By contrast, _____

Building a Norman castle was not a very skilful job. By contrast, _____

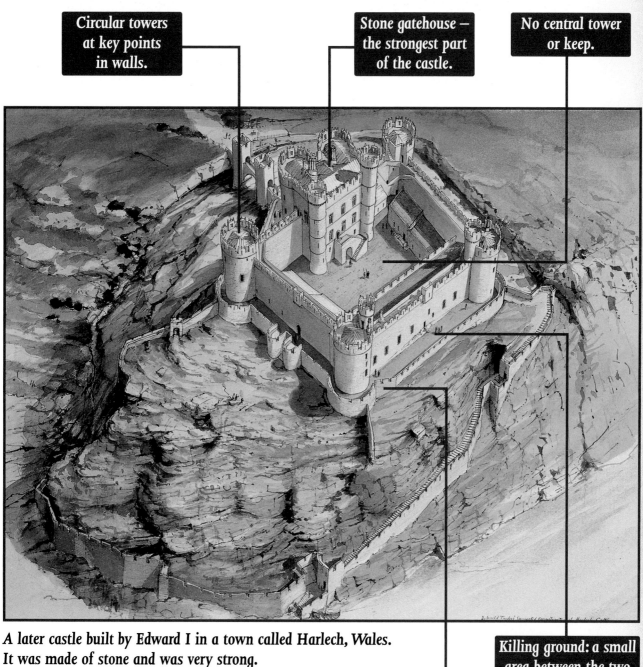

Circular towers at key points in walls.

Stone gatehouse — the strongest part of the castle.

No central tower or keep.

A later castle built by Edward I in a town called Harlech, Wales.
It was made of stone and was very strong.

Killing ground: a small area between the two walls where attackers would be trapped.

Stone walls.

---

2 Can you find any other contrasts between the castles? Write out your findings in the same style as the answers to Question 1 using the phrase 'by contrast' to link your sentences.

3 Are there any similarities between the early Norman castles and Edward's castles? Make a list of any you can find.

You Decide

4 You are a Welsh spy who has just visited the site of the new castle at Harlech in disguise. You have been sent to see if it is possible to attack the castle. Write a report saying what you think.

Royal murder mysteries:

The poster on this page is for the film Braveheart. The film tells the story of a war between the Scots and the English in the Middle Ages. The Scots were led by William Wallace. The English leader was King Edward I.

At first things went well for Wallace. He defeated an English army at Stirling Bridge in 1297 and drove the English out of Scotland. Later, his luck turned. Edward marched north and the two men came face to face at the Battle of Falkirk in 1298. Wallace was defeated but he managed to escape. Many of the Scots then surrendered but Wallace continued to fight against Edward. In 1305 Wallace was captured and taken to London where he was put to death by Edward.

A poster for the film Braveheart showing Mel Gibson playing the part of William Wallace (the leader of the Scots army).

1 The picture shows Wallace, as played by the movie star, Mel Gibson. Films often have heroes and villains: 'goodies' and 'baddies'. How can you tell from this picture that Wallace is the hero of the film?

2 The film was made in 1994, many hundreds of years after the death of Wallace. Did people at the time of the war think that Wallace was a hero? Look at these two sources which are descriptions of William Wallace. One source was written by an English monk and the other was written by a Scottish writer. Can you work out which writer was Scottish and which writer was English?

Source 1:

'Wallace was a merciless robber, an attacker of churches and a murderer. He was one of the cruellest men in all history. He burnt alive his enemies in schools and churches. He ran away from his own men at Falkirk and left them to be killed by the English. He was a man of the Devil who did wicked deeds beyond counting.'

Source 2:

'He was generous, fair, kind to those in trouble, a skilful leader, and a good speaker. He hated lies and for this reason God was on his side, and with His help, he was very successful. He cared for the Church and respected the clergy. He helped the poor and widows. He attacked thieves and robbers. God was very pleased with him.'

the death of William Wallace

In the film, Braveheart, Edward I is shown as an evil, ruthless man who murdered Wallace in cold-blood. If this happened today, Edward would be put on trial to decide whether or not he was guilty of murder. The jury would hear all the events before making their decision.

You Decide

3 Let's put Edward on trial for the murder of Wallace. You are the jury and must decide whether or not he was guilty. Look at each of the arguments on this page: the case for the prosecution and the case for the defence. Which one is more convincing? Explain your decision.

Edward on Trial for Murder

The case for the prosecution

When two countries go to war soldiers must fight by rules. This was true in the Middle Ages and it is true today. Edward did not fight by the rules and he was ready to use murder to get his way. Wallace was not the only Scot to be murdered by this man. When Edward stormed the town of Berwick in 1296 he said that all the Scottish men of the town should be killed. Thousands of men were put to death.

When Wallace was captured he should have been treated with respect as a prisoner-of-war. Instead he was brutally murdered after an unconvincing trial. The trial of Wallace was a joke. Wallace was not allowed to say anything in his defence. He was horribly tortured before his head was chopped off. His body was then chopped in four and sent to different parts of the country. This was murder.

The case for the defence

Let's get a few things clear. Edward did kill Wallace but it was not murder. Edward saw himself as the lord of Scotland. To him the Scots were not people of a separate country; they were his people and he was their lord. So any Scots who fought against him were rebels and traitors.

In the Middle Ages being a traitor against your lord was a terrible crime and the punishment was death. That's why Edward killed the men at Berwick who fought against him and that's why he executed Wallace. The way Wallace was treated was similar to the way other people were treated when they were accused of being traitors.

The problems faced by monarchs

As we saw at the beginning of this section, some kings and queens were successful at ruling and some were not. Successful monarchs were liked by their people and became rich. Unsuccessful monarchs were very unpopular and were often overthrown and killed.

1 You are helping a famous historian who has been invited to write a magazine article entitled: **What problems did medieval monarchs face?** The article has been partly written and she wants you to help her finish it off. She tells you what she wants you to do:

> 'I want each paragraph to start with a sentence about a particular problem. I've done the first three. Can you add some examples of when this problem happened?'

Women rulers faced more problems than men. _____

The Church was a problem because some Church leaders did not like taking orders from kings. _____

Monarchs had a major problem if they argued with their barons. _____

2 Look at the following sentences. Can you use any of the information statements in the paragraphs? Two of the sentences are irrelevant – can you spot them?

◆ Kings and queens travelled a lot.

◆ King Henry II had a terrible argument with Archbishop Thomas Becket.

◆ Medieval men had little respect for women; they thought women were inferior to men.

◆ Barons had their own private armies and could use these to fight against the monarch.

◆ Matilda was brave and clever but she was not able to rule over England.

◆ King John annoyed his barons so they went to war against him.

◆ Many children died before they became adults.

◆ Church leaders annoyed kings by saying that people in the Church should get special treatment if they broke the law.

3 Look back at earlier work you have done on kings and queens. Can you find any extra information to add to each paragraph? Can you find any more problems to put in the magazine article?

4 a The historian also wants you to help with her picture research. You have found two pictures of medieval life but you only have room in the magazine for one of them. The picture must be relevant to the article. Which picture do you think she should use? Why?

b Write a caption for the picture explaining what is happening in it.

A medieval picture of the death of Thomas Becket

A 19th century picture of King John and the barons

The power of religion

In thousands of towns and villages in Britain the only medieval buildings remaining are churches. Medieval churches can also be found all over Europe. They have survived because they are built of stone. Most medieval houses and farm buildings have not survived because they were made of wood, which rotted away over time. The churches were built to last because religion was very important to medieval people and Church leaders had lots of money to pay for stone buildings.

When is the Church not a church?

◆ We all know the word *church*, meaning the building. In this book we also use the word *Church*, with a capital C, to mean the organisation – the Archbishops, the Bishops and all the clergy, monks and nuns who led and organised the religious aspects of medieval life.

◆ In medieval times the only big religion in Britain was Catholic Christianity.

In this section of the book we will find out more about the Church and why it mattered so much to medieval people. As you learn more about religion and the Church make a note of all the ways in which the Church was important.

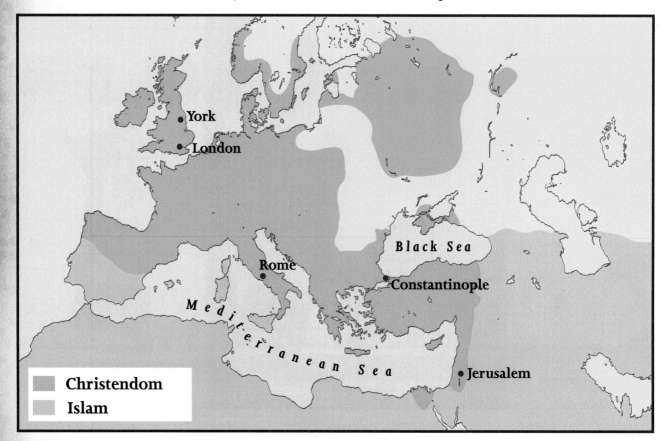

York
London
Rome
Black Sea
Constantinople
Mediterranean Sea
Jerusalem

Christendom
Islam

The heretic test: will you be burnt alive?

In 1401, the government of England introduced a new law ordering that all heretics should be burnt to death. *A **heretic*** was someone who disagreed with the teachings of the Church. Church leaders taught people how to be religious and what to believe. Anybody who questioned these teachings was called a heretic.

---

1 By a strange accident, you have been transported back to 1401. The church leaders think you look odd with your modern clothes, and they have put you on trial as a heretic. If you give the wrong answers to their questions (A–C) you will be burnt alive! Good luck!

A Would it be a good idea to have the Bible in English as well as the old language Latin?

Yes, we should have the Bible in the language people speak as well as the old language.

No, we should keep the Bible just in the old language to show what a special book it is. There is no reason to change it.

B Abbeys where monks and nuns live have got lots of land and are very rich. Should we close them down and give the money to the poor?

Yes, it's stupid letting monks and nuns have lots of wealth when we could do something better with the money.

No, leave the monks and nuns alone. They are very holy people and need the money to pay for their holy way of life.

C Some churches have the bones of dead, holy people on display. Is this a good idea?

No, it would be more sensible to bury the bones and not distract people from their prayers.

Yes, the bones of these holy people can help people when they pray to God.

Your teacher is the judge. If you have got one or more answers wrong you are a heretic and the punishment is… **death by burning.**

The Church is everywhere

In the Middle Ages the Church was very powerful. Church leaders were involved with other things besides preaching sermons to the people. Some helped the government to run the country, while some studied subjects like science and came up with new ideas. Some church leaders set up schools and hospitals.

Running the country

In Medieval times very few people could read and write. The Church was the only organisation that had lots of well-educated people. If people wanted to get letters written they would ask a priest to do it for them. The royal government needed people who could write to help run the country so they gave these jobs to men who were members of the Church.

The world of knowledge

As the only people who could read, priests were the only ones who could find out about different subjects like science, history and geography. So, people who were very interested in these subjects had to become priests, monks or nuns.

In those days books were unusual and rare because there was no printing. The monasteries and cathedrals had the only large collections of books. Priests and monks copied books by hand, and organised them into libraries.

Some priests set up schools to help educate people. Most poor people didn't go to school because they worked on the land. Schools were for richer children who didn't need to work and had time to learn.

Helping those in trouble

The government did almost nothing to help people who were poor. These people relied instead on the Church. The government did nothing to help sick people either. Medieval hospitals were all run by the Church. The Church was supposed to give a lot of its money to the poor. So if you had money troubles your best way of getting help was to ask a priest, monk or nun.

A hospital run by the monks. In the Middle Ages almost all hospitals belonged to the church.

Lots of land

The Church was very rich as it was the biggest landowner. When people wanted to give a big gift to the Church, they often gave land. As a result, priests, monks and nuns spent a lot of time as landlords, working with farmers and making sure that the land was being looked after properly.

---

1 Look at all these medieval people. They each have a problem or a need. In every case the Church can help them. Can you explain to each of these people how the Church can help them. Write a sentence for each telling them what they should do. Who would you ask for help for each of these problems today?

Thomas: *'I am interested in science. How can I find a job that will let me find out about the world?'*

Eleanor: *'I'm desperate. I've got no money, no job and two babies to feed.'*

George: *'I can read but I can't afford to buy any books. Is there a library around here?'*

Henry: *'I want some land so that I can be a farmer and can feed my family.'*

James: *'I'd like my children to go to school.'*

Anne: *'My old mother is very ill. She needs to be looked after in a hospital.'*

Adam: *'I'd like to work as a civil servant.'*

Eleanor
Adam
Anne
George
Henry
James
Thomas

Welcome to Hell

It's Sunday morning. Everyone in the village goes to church. The priest leads the service known as the Mass. It's in an old language called Latin so most people don't really understand what he's saying but they know that it is important and holy. One part of the service is always in English. This is the sermon. During the sermon the priest teaches people how to behave. They are told about all the sins that God dislikes. The priest tells people that some sins are very serious, and that sinners will be punished in Hell after they have died. Some of these medieval sermons have survived so we can find out what the priests said.

'Some people spend all their lives looking for pleasure and do nothing to help others. They will go to Hell. Each pleasure will be turned into a torture. Instead of scented baths, they shall have baths of burning tar. Instead of soft beds, they will lie on beds of nails and spikes. Instead of being kissed by beautiful lips, they will be embraced by burning hot irons.'

'People should dread the Day of Judgement and the **horrible pains** of Hell. All men and women will stand before God and be judged. Under Him the horrible pit of Hell will open up to take the sinners. On the left side of God will stand countless devils who will drive the sinners to the pains of Hell. Inside Hell is a world of **fire and burning**. There is no hiding place there for sinners. The sinners will be naked, covered only by **fire and filth**. Their only sights will be **darkness and smoke**. The only sounds **groaning and grinding of teeth**. Their nostrils will be always full of a **terrible stink**.'

The inside of a medieval church was covered with colourful wall paintings and statues. Ordinary people could not read and write but they could see the teachings of the Church in these paintings and statues. Above the main arch of the church building was a huge 'doom' painting. This showed God judging everybody and sending them either to Heaven or Hell.

Look at these medieval pictures of people in Hell. As the priest spoke about Hell he would point to pictures like this.

These illustrations of Hell show sinners being showered by a rain of fire, coffins containing the heads of heretics and sinners head first in boiling barrels of tar.

1 Explain in your own words what medieval people thought about Hell.

2 The sermons and pictures are both meant to frighten people. Which do you think are more frightening?

3 Underline some words in the sermons that tell you that Hell is a frightening place.

4 Why might the Church want people to be afraid?

How to get to Heaven

Medieval people were understandably frightened at the idea of Hell. They wanted to go to Heaven. Priests preached that Heaven was a wonderful place where nobody had any troubles. People all wanted to know how to get to Heaven and how to avoid going to Hell. They asked their priests what they should do and how they should behave. This is the answer that one priest gave:

'God could have made all people strong and rich. He decided not to. Instead he wished that some should be strong and others weak, some should be rich and others poor. For if all were strong and rich there would be no one to help. And if all were weak and poor, no one would be able to do anything to help others. God made some people strong and rich so that they could get to heaven by helping others. He made others weak and poor so that they could get to heaven by putting up with their troubles without complaining.'

Ralph of Acton

Priests also said that there were seven deadly sins. They were deadly because if you did them a lot God would send you straight to Hell. If you wanted to go to Heaven you first had to avoid these seven deadly sins:

◆ **Pride:** thinking that you are better than other people.

◆ **Envy:** wanting things that other people have got.

◆ **Gluttony:** eating and drinking too much.

◆ **Lust:** thinking too much about sex.

◆ **Anger:** losing your temper in a violent way.

◆ **Covetousness:** thinking too much about money and wealth.

◆ **Sloth:** being too lazy.

Gluttony was one of the seven deadly sins. This person is vomiting because he is guilty of gluttony – he has eaten too much.

Copy a saint

Priests also used the example of saints to show how people could get to Heaven. Saints were holy people who had been very good and had behaved in the right way. People were sure that when saints died they went to Heaven. By copying what saints did during their lives, people hoped to reach Heaven too. Each church had lots of pictures and statues of different saints. Let's look at the pictures of a saint called Louis. He was very religious and he did everything that priests told him to do.

Punish yourself

In this picture Saint Louis allows a monk to flog him. Priests said that God was pleased when men and women punished themselves for their sins to show how sorry they were. One way of saying sorry was by whipping yourself regularly or getting a friend to whip you. Another way of punishing yourself was by wearing a hair-shirt (which was a very uncomfortable, itchy vest that you wore under your clothes).

Help the Church

Here Louis visits an abbey and works as a waiter to a sick priest. Priests had special powers. God listened to their prayers. By giving gifts to priests and monks people could help them with their holy work. In return for these gifts priests said prayers for their friends. By helping this sick priest Louis knew that he was pleasing God.

Look after the poor

Louis washes the feet of some poor men. Priests said that people should help each other and should especially help those with problems. Washing the dirty, smelly feet of some local beggars was one good way of pleasing God. Afterwards the poor men were given food and money. Some saints tried to give away all their money to the poor.

---

1 Medieval people believed that they could get into Heaven by doing the right things. Make a list for a medieval person, using the information from this unit.

My Checklist for Heaven

I must
- ◆
- ◆
- ◆
- ◆
- ◆

I must not
- ◆
- ◆
- ◆
- ◆
- ◆

Monks and Nuns

Monasteries were very important places in the Middle Ages. Inside monasteries monks and nuns were supposed to follow very strict rules. Despite this, many people wanted to join them.

What was life like for monks and nuns?

Monks and nuns were not allowed to get married.

Monks did interesting work as writers, doctors and book illustrators.

Kings, queens and other famous people were friends with monks and nuns. These celebrities often stayed at monasteries.

Ordinary monks and nuns spent a long time in church. There were at least eight services that they had to attend every day.

There was a chance of promotion to a powerful job. If you became abbot or abbess (the most important monk or nun in the monastery) you could be one of the most powerful people in the country.

The abbot or abbess had total power. A monk or nun who disobeyed could be beaten or locked up and put in chains.

Bedtime was about seven o'clock and monks and nuns got up at two o'clock in the morning.

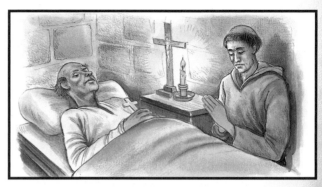

People thought that monks and nuns had a better chance than anyone else of going to heaven.

There was only one meal a day during summer and meat was forbidden except during illness.

Nuns did skilful artistic work as embroiderers.

Monks (but not nuns) were given a first class education.

Private property was not allowed. Monks and nuns were supposed to share everything.

Look back at the information on these pages.

1 Can you find any information that suggests that monks and nuns lived lives of hardship?

2 Can you find any information that explains why many people wanted to become monks or nuns?

Which order should I join?

If you wanted to become a monk or a nun, you had to join a religious order. These orders were groups of people who lived by certain rules and served God. Some orders were much more strict than others.

> **1** A group of medieval people have asked you for advice. They all want to join a religious order but you must make sure that they join the one that suits them best. Match each person to a different order.

Name: Thomas *'Most religious orders are too soft. I want a really strict order so I can be sure of getting into Heaven when I die. The world is a wicked place and I want to get far away from ordinary people so I can concentrate on God.'*

Name: Joan *'I want to devote myself completely to God's work. I like the ideas of St Francis who says we must give up everything to be like Jesus. Of course, as a woman, I cannot copy Francis and wander from place to place. But I can hide myself away and spend my life in prayer.'*

Name: Henry *'I'm torn between wanting a life of prayer as a monk and wanting to help people in trouble. I'm very religious but I'm also interested in medicine and looking after the sick. Is there an order that will help me to keep up my interest in both these things?'*

Name: James *'I don't even know if they'll have me in a monastery. I come from a poor family and I can't read or write. I like doing practical things like farming and building work. I'd like to help better educated monks in their holy work.'*

Name: Matthew *'I don't want to be locked away in a monastery. I want to be out in the world talking to ordinary people about Jesus. I don't want to join a really rich order because followers of Jesus should have no money.'*

Name: Matilda *'I want to serve God but I'm not a religious fanatic. I like prayers but I don't want to be in church all day and all night. I like nice food and good company. To be honest, I'm a bit of a snob and I only feel at home with other ladies like me from the top families of the land.'*

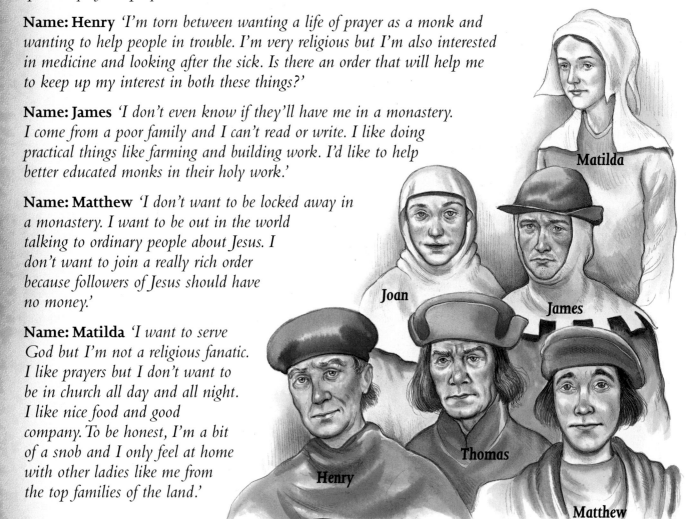

Matilda

Joan

James

Thomas

Henry

Matthew

Benedictine Nuns

Upper class ladies only need apply.

As the oldest and wealthiest order of nuns, we are quite choosy about new members. We particularly welcome new nuns from royal and noble families. Life here is not too strict. You will spend some of your time in church but you can also spend time talking to friends and doing hobbies like embroidery.

Cistercian Lay Brothers

Are you poor, badly educated, unemployed but keen on religion?

We have the right place for you. Even poor men are welcome as Cistercian Lay Brothers. You do not need to be able to read but you will have to work very hard helping the Cistercian monks around the monastery and on their farms. You will serve the monks and will help them to carry out their holy work.

Poor Clares Nuns

You don't have to be called Clare to join us but if you join you will be very poor!

We are named after Saint Clare, the sister of Saint Francis. Like her brother she wanted to copy Jesus by living a simple life and giving away all her money. As a Poor Clare you will never leave your monastery and will spend nearly all your time praying.

Augustinian Canons

You want to be a monk but you also want to get out and help people.
The Augustinians could be the answer to your prayers. Our members are known as canons because they're different from ordinary monks. They spend a lot of time in church but they also help local people and run a number of hospitals.

Franciscan Friars

Want to see the world
AND
get to Heaven?

Life as a friar could be right for you. With us you will have an interesting and varied life. You will go from place to place preaching to people. Our order was founded by the Italian, Saint Francis. He believed that we should give all we have to the poor.

Cistercian Monks

Want to get away from it all?

We offer a strict life in monasteries set in wild remote countryside. You will hardly ever see other people and this will help you to concentrate on your life as a monk. This is the life for the monk who is really serious about getting to Heaven.

---

1 *Give each order a score out of ten depending on how strict it was. Which was the most strict? Which was the least strict?*

2 *'Not all monasteries were the same.' Would you agree with this? Use information from this page to help you answer.*

Religion and the law

The Church influenced almost every part of life in medieval times, including how criminals were judged. Criminals could hide in a church and claim protection (*sanctuary*) from their enemies. There were special church courts too, where priests were put on trial. Religion also influenced how a criminal was punished. People believed that if a criminal was tested, God would decide whether the criminal was innocent or guilty and whether they lived or died.

Sanctuary

Criminals could not be arrested if they were able to reach a church because once they were inside the church they were under God's protection. This was called seeking sanctuary. Those who stayed in the church for forty days without leaving were allowed to go free, provided they then left the country immediately. Anyone who failed to leave the country, or returned to England later, was hanged. Occasionally people were dragged out of churches by their enemies when they were seeking sanctuary. This was seen as a great crime against God.

Church courts

Priests and church leaders were given special privileges and were tried by their own special church courts. These were much less strict than other courts. Priests and other clergy could not be executed. If a priest killed a man (which happened surprisingly often) they might be ordered to go on a pilgrimage to Rome or Jerusalem. The Church also had its own prisons which were more easy-going than royal prisons.

Above: Monks are caught in bed with women. When monks and priests broke the law they were tried by their own special church courts.

Do you remember how Henry II argued with Archbishop Thomas Becket? Henry wanted to stop the special treatment of priests who had committed crimes. He failed to do this and criminal priests continued to get away with murder. Many criminals actually pretended that they were priests to try to avoid strict punishment.

---

1 Explain in your own words how criminals could escape punishment by seeking sanctuary.

2 In what way did priests who broke the law get special treatment?

3 How does the system of sanctuary and church courts show that the Church was important?

Let God decide...

Religion was important in law and order. If there was no clear-cut evidence of guilt, people expected God to let them know who was guilty. This was done by testing the criminal by one of the different **ordeals** (trials) below:

Trial by Fire

A suspect was given a red-hot iron to hold and told to walk a set number of paces. The hand was then bandaged. It was examined a few days later. If there was blistering and burnt skin this was a sign from God that the suspect was guilty and should be hanged.

Trial by Water

Accused people were bound and thrown into a river or stream. If they floated this was a sign from God that they were guilty and they were hanged. If they sank they needed to be rescued quickly to avoid drowning.

Trial by Combat

If one person accused another they were sometimes forced to fight each other. If the accused person lost the battle this was a sign from God that they were guilty and were hanged. People who were unwell or weak had to find a replacement who would fight on their behalf.

The ordeal of the bier

In cases of murder, suspects were sometimes taken to the body as it lay on a special table known as a bier. If the suspect was guilty the wounds on the dead person would open and bleed. The suspect was then hanged.

One way of letting God decide the fate of the accused was trial by combat. The loser was guilty and often dead.

You $Decide$

4 You are living in a medieval village and you have been wrongly accused of murder. The evidence is not clear so it has been decided that God must decide. You can choose one ordeal (trial) in order to prove your innocence. Which of the four ordeals would you choose? Explain your answer.

Let's go on pilgrimage

Travelling in the medieval times was not easy. The roads were poor. There was a high risk of attack from robbers. Often there was nowhere to stay at night. Despite this, many people chose to go on long journeys to visit holy places. These journeys were called **pilgrimages,** and were very difficult. People went on pilgrimages if they were very religious or if they needed to make up for a lot of sins. Some of these travellers (known as **pilgrims**) walked hundreds of miles with bare feet.

Why did people go on pilgrimage?

Some people went on pilgrimages to places in Britain. Others went much further and travelled to places like Rome and Jerusalem. At the end of the journey they visited a church. Once inside the church the pilgrims said prayers at a little chapel called a shrine. This contained the bones or other remains of a saint (known as relics). The most popular pilgrimage centre in England was Canterbury Cathedral. Here pilgrims could pray before the bones of Thomas Becket who was made a saint after his death. Let's visit medieval Canterbury and ask a monk to explain what happened.

'A saint like Thomas is a holy person who has died and lives now with God in Heaven. When you are at a shrine you are close to the saint. Your prayers here have special power and strength. The saint in Heaven looks down and listens to you and may be able to help you with your problems. Afterwards we expect visitors to give a gift of money to us. If you give a large gift we may take the head of the saint out of its case and let you kiss it.'

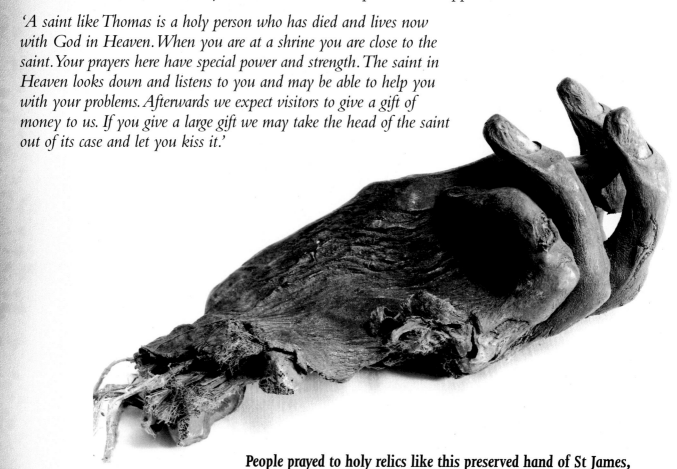

People prayed to holy relics like this preserved hand of St James, which can be seen today in a church in Buckinghamshire.

Now let's meet some pilgrims and find out why they've come to Canterbury:

Name: Robert *'I have done some very bad things in my life: stealing, fighting, cheating. My priest says he can't forgive me until I go on a pilgrimage as a punishment.'*

Name: John *'I was at sea when a terrible storm started. I thought, "This is it. I'm going to drown". I said, "Saint Thomas, save me and I promise to make a pilgrimage to your shrine at Canterbury". The storm died down and I was saved.'*

Name: Agnes *'I've had a bad leg now for years. I've tried everything. The doctors are hopeless and their medicine does nothing. I'm hoping for a miracle cure. I hear that many sick people have been cured by praying at the shrine of Saint Thomas.'*

Name: Mary *'I'm getting old now and I want to make sure I go to Heaven when I die. I don't want to be tortured forever in hell. Going on pilgrimage will help. God will be pleased with me for making the effort and will let me join him in Heaven.'*

1 Match these motives to the pilgrims:
   ◆ hoping for a miracle
   ◆ punishment for sins
   ◆ saying thank you to a saint for a favour or a promise
   ◆ a way of pleasing God and getting into Heaven.

2 Design a poster encouraging people to go on pilgrimage to Canterbury. Explain what happens at Canterbury and all the benefits that you can get from such a pilgrimage.

3 Imagine you are a pilgrim travelling to Canterbury. Write a paragraph (about 6 or 7 lines) describing what happened to you when you arrived at the shrine. How did you feel? What did you see? Who did you meet?

A pilgrimage was supposed to be a holy journey that people took very seriously. Some people were very religious, but people had other reasons for making the journey too. We know from documents written at the time that some pilgrims thought that going on a pilgrimage meant that they could behave how they liked. For them it was more of a holiday.

Source 1: from an anonymous story called *The Tale of Sir Beryn*, written in about 1400

What to do when you arrive at your destination: Find a pub

'Some pilgrims arrived at Canterbury and first of all went to an inn. One pilgrim went straight to the taproom where the beer and wine was served. The barmaid cried 'You are welcome, brother.' She said this with a very friendly look, as if she wanted a kiss. He wasted no time but grabbed her by the middle and gave her a kiss as if he had known her for years. They started talking and she told him that she was sad because her boyfriend had died recently. He tried to cheer her up. He said his name was Jenken. She replied that she was called Kit. Jenken looked Kit straight in the face in a loving way. He sighed and began to sing a song called 'Now, love, do me right'.

Some pilgrims treated a pilgrimage like a holiday: they danced and had a good time.

Source 2: from *The Book of Margery Kempe*, written in 1436, by Margery Kempe herself. Margery was from King's Lynn. She frequently went on pilgrimage and wrote a book about her life and travels.

What to do when you arrive at your destination: Find a church

'When I finally reached Jerusalem I thanked God for letting me see this marvellous place. I was so happy to be in the holy city that I fainted. Two Dutch pilgrims saved me from falling off my donkey. It was evening and we went straight to the Temple church and stayed there all night and most of the next day. Then we toured the city with monks who showed us all the places where Jesus had been. When I heard about the sufferings of Jesus I wept and sobbed. When we reached Calvary where Jesus died I was so upset I could not stand up.'

Source 3: William Thorpe speaking in 1407. He was a heretic who was on trial for not agreeing with the Catholic Church. He said these things about pilgrims during his trial.

Enjoy yourself on the way and make new friends!

'It is more for the health of their bodies, than of their souls! It is more to make friends with other people than to have friendship of God and of His saints in Heaven. Foolish people waste money on these silly pilgrimages, handing over cash to greedy innkeepers instead of giving charity to the poor. They would be better off staying at home and looking after their poor needy neighbours. They enjoy themselves, and annoy other people, by singing rude songs as they go along and playing bagpipes. In every town that they come through, what with the noise of their singing, and with the sound of their piping, and with the barking out of dogs after them, they make more noise than if the King had come to town. A few start with good intentions, but after six months they are like all the rest.'

1 Read each source carefully:

a In each case, decide why people went on a pilgrimage: for religious reasons or to have a good time.

b Note down any evidence that supports your view.

c Do you think we can trust each of these sources as evidence of why people went on a pilgrimage?

	Why they went	Evidence	Can we trust the source?
Source 1:			
Source 2:			
Source 3:			

The perils of pilgrimage

The bravest pilgrims went all the way to Jerusalem, where Jesus lived and was crucified. Today we can fly to Jerusalem in four hours. In medieval times the journey across land and sea took up to a year. William Wey, a 15th century English teacher, wrote a guide book for pilgrims who wanted to go to Jerusalem, giving them advice on the perils of pilgrimage.

Where to stay:

Do a deal with the owner of a galley in Venice. Make sure that you get a place on the top deck for in the lowest it is right smouldering hot and stinking. To get a good place and be looked after you will need to pay 40 gold coins for your boat trip and back again to Venice. Buy a feather bed, a mattress, two pillows, two pair of sheets, and a quilt.

What to take:

Take with you three 10 gallon barrels, two full of wine and one with water. Keep these for emergencies as the ship's captain should give you wine and water and feed you twice a day. Take another barrel with you to use as a toilet for your room in the galley. When you call into ports beware of the fruit, for if you are not used to them they can lead to diarrhoea. If an Englishman gets that sickness, it is a marvel not to die of it.

What to eat:

Take a large wooden chest for your things. Put a lock and key on your chest. Sailors and other pilgrims will try to steal from you. In your chest keep supplies of bread, cheese, spices, and other food. For though the captain will give you food, sometimes it will be stale bread, sour wine, and stinking water. Then you will want to go away and eat on your own. Take a little pot and frying-pan and other dishes for your own cooking. Buy a bird-cage and half a dozen hens, and buy millet seed to feed them.

Once you get there:

Stay in the Holy Land thirteen or fourteen days. Look after your knives and other small things that you carry with you, for the Saracens are friendly but they will steal from you what you have if they can. When you ride out from Jerusalem to the River Jordan, take with you bread, wine, water, hard cheese, and boiled eggs, enough for two days, for there is none for sale on the way.

Avoid illness:

And if you go out to the desert where our Lord Jesus Christ fasted forty days and forty nights, it is very hot. When you come back, make sure you drink no water, but rest a little, and then eat bread and drink clean wine without water. In that great heat, water starts a great diarrhoea or fever, or both; then you can easily die.

1 Make a list of all the things that William Wey thinks pilgrims should take. Explain why each of these things was important.

2 Make a list of all the things that could go wrong on the journey to Jerusalem.

3 'The source shows that getting to Jerusalem was difficult. People would only go if they were very religious.' Do you agree with this statement?

Chaucer and the Church

Let's try to find out what one man called Geoffrey Chaucer thought about the Church. He was a writer, and his most famous book was called The Canterbury Tales. At the beginning of his book he gives descriptions of some typical medieval people on a pilgrimage to Canterbury. The pilgrims tell the story of their journey. The characters in the book include some people working for the Church: a prioress (nun), a monk and a parson (priest). We can try to work out what Chaucer thought about the Church by looking at his descriptions of these three pilgrims.

Chaucer had to be very careful what he said about the Church because if he was too critical he might be called a heretic. The penalty for being a heretic was death. He got round this by not talking about the Church in general but by describing some particular people who worked for the Church: nuns, monks and priests. Before you look at Chaucer's descriptions, you need to remember the rules that nuns, monks and priests were supposed to obey.

Rules for people working for the Church

- Live in a very strict and simple way.
- Wear cheap plain clothes and do not try to look good.
- Eat very little meat.
- Spend your time on holy activities: praying, preaching and looking after other people.
- Have very few things of your own and give any spare money or food to the poor.

> **1** Now look at Chaucer's pilgrims. For each one decide whether they were following the rules.

The Prioress

- She regularly ate meat.

- She owned some little dogs and gave them the finest food.

- She wore very stylish clothes.

- She had lots of jewellery, including a coral bracelet, green beads and a golden brooch.

The Monk

- He spent most of his time hunting.

- He had a large collection of fine horses.

- He disliked studying or working in the fields.

- His clothes were trimmed with the finest fur.

- He loved food and his favourite meat was whole roasted swan.

The Parson

- He spent almost all his time preaching and teaching local people.

- He was generous and gave much of his own money to the poor.

- He made sure to visit people when they were sick or in trouble to see if he could help and comfort them.

- He looked after everybody whether they were rich or poor.

- He thought nothing of walking great distances in bad weather to visit families in isolated cottages.

2 Here are three general statements about the Church. Which one do you think Chaucer would agree with?
- People in the Church were doing a great job.
- People in the Church were a disgrace.
- Some people in the Church were a disgrace but some were doing a great job.

3 Write a paragraph answering the question "What did Chaucer think about the Church?" Make sure your paragraph makes a main point and has some supporting details. Try to use the word 'however' to show that the answer is a complex one.

Why were the Jews mistreated?

Today people of many faiths live in Britain: Christians, Muslims, Hindus, Jews, Buddhists. In Medieval times it was different. Almost everyone was Christian. The one exception was a small group of Jewish people. They were very badly treated by the Christians.

Let's look at what happened to the Jews of York in 1190.

The story of the Jews of York

A leading Jew called Benedict died, in York, in March 1190. A gang of local people broke into the dead man's house. They killed his widowed wife and his children and stole all his money. The gang attacked other Jewish families, beating and robbing them. As a result, all the Jews in York fled to the royal castle. In the past, the king had protected them. However, the king was out of the country and there was no one who would help them.

This is an artist's impression of York castle on fire after the Jews had committed suicide.

The Jews barricaded themselves in the castle. They were surrounded by an armed Christian mob led by Richard Malebisse. Like many of the leaders of the mob, Malebisse had money problems and he owed a lot of money to some of the Jews. The mob burned all the records of money owed to the Jews so that they didn't have to pay it back.

The Jews knew that they could not stay in the castle forever. They were sure that the mob were going to murder them in a brutal way. The Jewish rabbi (a leader of the Jewish Church) made a grim decision. He told all the Jews that to escape being captured by the Christians they must commit suicide. Each man killed his own wife and children. The rabbi then killed the men and set fire to the castle, before killing himself.

---

1 *Are there any clues in the story as to why the Jews of York were so badly treated?*

2 *How can you tell from the story that the Jews were terrified of their Christian neighbours?*

The tragic events in York were just one example of how Christians mistreated Jews. They were repeatedly attacked and discriminated against. Finally, in 1290, they were forced to leave England. Why were they so badly treated? Let's look at a number of factors why people mistreated Jews:

Did the Church encourage people to mistreat the Jews?

Factor 1: Priests told people that Jewish people were wicked. Priests blamed Jews for the death of Jesus, even though he had died hundreds of years before and he was himself a Jew. The Church ordered that all Jewish people must wear special signs on their clothes. This made it easier for people to insult Jews on the street and to beat them up.

Did kings encourage people to mistreat the Jews?

Factor 2: Jewish people depended on the king to protect them. Many kings, such as Henry II, did try to stop violence against the Jews. Other kings did very little to help the Jews. Henry III and his son, Edward I, hated Jewish people. During the reign of kings like this people knew that they could attack Jews and get away with their crimes. In 1290, Edward I ordered all Jews to leave England.

Did ignorance encourage people to mistreat the Jews?

Factor 3: Christians and Jews lived and worked completely separately. Strange, untrue rumours went round among Christians about what Jews were like. The most awful rumour was that the Jews sometimes carried out the human sacrifice of young Christian boys. This was complete nonsense but many people knew so little about Jews that they believed it.

3 *Answer each of the questions above.*

4 *Which of these three factors do you think was the most important cause of the Jews being mistreated?*

This picture shows Jewish people being attacked by a Christian in 1275. Can you see the special sign on the Jews' clothes? How did badges like this encourage attacks on Jews?

Was the Church doing its job well?

Historians disagree about the Church in later medieval times. Some say it was hopeless, others say it was doing a good job. Look at the information in this unit and see what you think.

> 1 Look at the following descriptions of the Church in medieval times. Decide whether each description supports the idea that the Church was doing its job well or doing its job badly.
>
> | The Church was doing its job well | The Church was doing its job badly |
> |---|---|
> | | |
>
> 2 Can you find one point that could be put in both columns?

Descriptions of the church

◆ There was a big increase in church building 1300–1500. Major building work took place in 75 per cent of the parish churches of England. Local people gave the money to pay for this building work.

◆ The rules for monasteries said that monks and nuns should only eat meat when they were sick. But most monks and nuns ate meat every day.

◆ Religious clubs called guilds became very popular among ordinary people. The number of these guilds increased greatly 1300–1500. Members were ordinary people who met at their local church to pray for dead friends and relatives.

◆ A group of people called Lollards said that that the Church was a waste of time and was too rich. Lollards believed that praying to saints and relics was useless. Most people did not join the Lollards. Most people continued to believe in what the Church said about saints and relics.

◆ Printing reached Britain in the late 1400s. More and more people could read and buy books . The best selling books were prayer books and other religious books.

◆ Very few new monasteries were set up in the late Middle Ages. The number of monks and nuns went down in many monasteries.

◆ There were frequent arguments about the payment of a tax called tithes to the Church. People did not see why they should have to give 10 per cent of all their income to the Church. Some farmers in Devon staged a protest. They took 10 per cent of all their milk to the local church and poured it on the ground in front of the priest.

The top picture shows a new, very strict monastery built by monks of the Carthusian order at the end of the Middle Ages. The bottom picture shows a monk and nun being punished for misbehaving.

3 Look at each of the pictures on this page. For each one decide whether it fits in with the idea of the Church doing its job badly, or doing its job well.

4 People sometimes disagree about the past because they select different information when they are deciding what life was like. Explain how you can reach a different view of what the Church was like depending on the information you select.

Why was the Church so important?

By now you've seen that the Church mattered a great deal to medieval people. It played a part in people's lives in many ways. Now it's your chance to look back at everything you've found out about the Church.

The owners of a ruined abbey are having a medieval 'living history' day. Actors dressed as medieval monks and nuns will show visitors around. They've heard about your work on medieval religion and they've asked you to help the actors by telling them all about the medieval Church and why it was so important.

1 The actors are very good at acting, but they don't know very much about history. They have lots of questions about medieval religion. Write a report describing religion in medieval times. Make sure that your report answers all the actors' questions. The actors are very busy so they only want a single A4 sheet that gives them the information they need.

'Most people don't go to church today. Why was it so different in medieval times? Why was the Church so rich and powerful then?'

'The life of a monk or a nun seems strange to me. Did they really spend all their time praying? Why did people want to become monks and nuns?'

'I hear that pilgrims used to visit this monastery. Who were these pilgrims and why did they go on pilgrimage?'

'Today we have many different faiths in Britain. Was Christianity the only faith in medieval Britain? If there were any other faiths, how were they treated by the Christians?'

Medieval people: did they have a hard life?

Most people in medieval Britain lived in the countryside. They farmed land belonging to their landlord. Some people lived in towns like London and York, which were very different to modern towns. In this section of the book you will find out about some of the difficulties faced by ordinary people.

In investigating how hard life really was you will have a chance to consider:

◆ Was it equally hard for people living in the countryside and people living in towns?

◆ Was life hard for all sections of society (villeins, landlords, merchants)?

◆ Did richer people reduce the hardships of poorer people by offering to help?

◆ What happened when people got fed up of the hardships?

Look at these two sources. Do they suggest that life was hard?

Source 1

'As I went by I saw a poor man ploughing. His toes stuck out of his worn shoes. He was covered with mud. The man sank up to his ankles in mud as he walked along. His plough was pulled by four heifers. They were so badly fed that you could count every rib. His wife walked beside him. She had an overcoat and a sheet to keep out the cold. She walked barefoot on the frozen ground and her feet were bleeding. At the end of the field was a baby covered in rags. Two older children were crying. The poor man sighed deeply and said, "Children, be quiet!"'

Source 1 is a quotation from a fourteenth-century poem called *The Vision of Piers Ploughman*. It paints a very sad picture of what life was like for ordinary people in medieval times. The life of these people is full of suffering.

Source 2 is a photo of country people spending their free time watching and betting on a cock-fight.

Source 2

In 1086, just before he died, William the Conqueror ordered the Normans to find out more about every place in England. The result was the Domesday Book, a massive description of England. He wanted the Domesday Book written so that he could work out who had money and who he could tax. William the Conqueror did not live to use it. His son, William Rufus took over as king in 1087.

Here is one entry from the Domesday Book.
It is a description of the village of Rayleigh in Essex:

'A baron called Suen has the village of Rayleigh. There are two families of slaves and twenty-one families of semi-slaves. There are no free families. As well as the land that is ploughed there are 10 acres of meadow for feeding animals, and woodland where pigs graze. There are 7 horses, 20 cattle, 11 pigs, 80 sheep and 11 goats. Suen gets £10 a year in rent from Rayleigh. He has built a park for hunting, a vineyard and a castle.'

There are thousands of entries like this. By putting them all together we can find out lots about what England was like at the time. Let's see what we can learn from the Domesday Book about different groups of people in England.

Fierce knights like this became landlords after the conquest.

Domesday evidence 1: Norman barons

There are 2 million people in England but over half the country belongs to just 200 Norman barons. 12 of William the Conqueror's special friends own a quarter of the country. In modern terms these men would be millionaires. Almost of all of these very rich landlords are men.

Domesday evidence 2: English landowners

Over 90 per cent of English landowners had their land taken off them after the Norman conquest. They had been rich and important but afterwards they were poor. Many of them now work as poor farmers for the new, rich Norman landlords.

Domesday evidence 3: The Church

The Church had lots of money and land before 1066. The Normans liked the Church and they gave it even more money and land. By the time of the Domesday Book the Church was the richest landowner in the country. Bishops and the top monks and nuns had huge incomes from their farms.

Domesday evidence 4: Ordinary English people

Most ordinary people were semi-slaves, working for their landlords on farms. They were known as villeins. They had very little money and only a few animals. Some were better off than others. In the east of England there were more free ordinary people. In the north of England hundreds of villages were in ruins at the time of the Domesday Book. These northern villages had been destroyed by William the Conqueror during 'the Harrying of the North'.

Domesday evidence 5: People of the towns

Except for London, towns were very small. Even important cities like Canterbury and Oxford only had a population of about 4000 people. Towns got poorer and smaller immediately after the Norman conquest. The Normans knocked down hundreds of houses in towns to build castles.

---

1 You work for the new king, William Rufus. He wants to know more about his kingdom. In particular, he wants to know who is rich in England because he wants to tax them. Write a report for William using the evidence from the Domesday Book.

The Domesday Book provides lots of interesting background information but it doesn't give a full picture of ordinary people's lives. We need to look at other types of sources, such as archaeological findings and medieval pictures, to see if they give us additional information about how people lived.

The archaeology of death

Archaeologists get their information from some very surprising places. Take, for example, cemeteries where dead people are buried. Over the last few years many medieval cemeteries have been investigated by archaeologists. The skeletons of medieval people can tell us a lot about their lives. The archaeologists have discovered that:

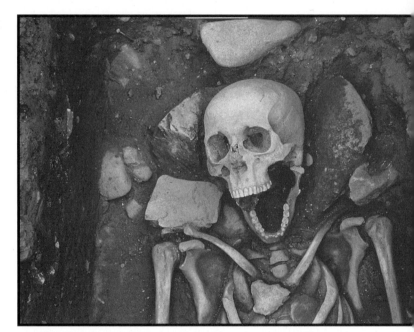

We know from looking at skeletons in graves that many medieval people died violent deaths. This man has been decapitated. His skull is no longer joined to his body.

◆ **People often died young in medieval times.** In one cemetery in Winchester there were 241 skeletons. Just over half of these were children. At one site in Hereford the average age at death of the men was 34 years. Women did not live as long as men. The average age of the women's skeletons was only 24 years. Many women probably died during childbirth.

◆ **Some bodies show signs of violence.** At St Andrew's cemetery in York, twenty-nine men had injuries caused by blades or daggers. Six of the men had been decapitated. At a cemetery in Norwich, some skeletons appear to be criminals who have been hanged. They had their wrists tied behind their backs and had been thrown in the burial pit face first.

◆ **The bones of children often show evidence of hunger.** Archaeologists can tell this from 'bone scars'. These are lines showing where children stopped growing because their bodies did not have enough food. The lines disappear later in life and can only be found on the bodies of children.

◆ **People were often ill or in pain.** At St Andrews in York, almost all the skeletons of people aged 50 or over had damaged joints. Arthritis was very common among older adults. At St Nicholas Shambles cemetery in London, many of the bodies had damaged backbones due to lifting too many heavy loads. Skeletons of men were four times more likely to have damaged backs than women.

Medieval pictures

Many medieval manuscripts and books had drawings in them depicting the lives of ordinary people. A manuscript called the Luttrell Psalter has some very good pictures of people working and entertaining themselves.

This illustration from the Luttrell Psalter manuscript shows a medieval person sowing seed in his field.

1 Look at all the archaeological sources and the pictures. What can you find out about people's everyday lives from these sources? Copy out this table and write down what you have discovered in the correct column.

Cemeteries	Luttrell Psalter

2 Can we learn anything from the sources about people's health?

3 Can we learn anything from the sources about the work people did?

4 What else can we learn from these sources about the lives of ordinary people?

Meet the villeins

Most ordinary medieval people lived in the countryside. Some were called villeins. They were semi-slaves who did not own any land and they had very few rights. They belonged to the lord and lady of the manor. What was life like for medieval villeins?

If you met some medieval villeins how would you find out about their lives? Hugh and Alice are villeins. They live in a small village where they work and live on 15 acres (0.15 hectares) of land. What questions would you ask them? Perhaps you would like to know:

What do you have to eat?

Do your children have to go to school?

Do you have a toilet in your house?

Are you cruel to animals?

What are your farms like?

What do you do when you're not working?

Hugh and Alice have given you these answers to your questions.

'We eat brown bread and drink ale. Only rich folk eat white bread. The ale is not very strong and we drink it all day, even at breakfast. Lords and ladies don't like ale. They say it's common. They drink wine instead. We don't eat much meat. Just some bacon as a treat sometimes. Every night we have a big vegetable stew called a pottage, with beans and onions. Rich people eat meat all the time. If you ask me they do it just to show us all how well off they are.'

'There is a school in the nearest town but our children aren't allowed to go there. We can't read and write. Mind you, not many people can, except for priests. There's no point going to school unless you want to go and work for the Church. Instead of wasting time reading, children start work as soon as they can. I don't know how we'd manage our land without the children.'

'I hear they have a special room in fancy houses called a garderobe or a privy. That's where the rich folk relieve themselves. We don't have anything like that in our houses. We use a pot or just go outside.'

'I wouldn't say we were cruel to animals but we do like watching a good cock-fight or bear-baiting. Of course, we're close to our own animals. Very close. You see they live in the other end of our longhouse. Smells a bit, but it helps to keep us warm. It's always a pity when we have to kill most of the animals around about November time. There's not a lot of food around for humans when it's winter, let alone extra food for animals.'

'We don't work all the time. No one works on Sunday – except the priest. We have twelve days holiday at Christmas. We have other holidays on a feast day for an important saint. When we get a chance, we play games like archery or wrestling. Women take turns at brewing beer and we have a celebration.'

This is a typical medieval villeins' house, like the one that Hugh and Alice would have lived in. It was made of timber and thatch and had one large room where everybody lived, cooked, ate and slept.

The house was made of wood. They burnt down very easily.

There was no chimney and few windows. The house was full of smoke.

There was no privacy as everyone lived in one room.

Animals shared the house with humans.

1 How many differences can you identify between the way villeins lived and the way we live today?

2 What information suggests that rich and poor people lived very differently in medieval times?

3 The peasants say that they are not cruel to animals. Do you agree with them?

4 From what you have read about Hugh and Alice's life, do you think that life was hard for them?

The power of the lord

Rich lords and ladies usually owned many manor houses and villages. They were often absent. Despite this they had a big impact on the daily lives of villeins.

What would you want to know about the lord who owned the villeins' village? Hugh can tell us all we need to know.

Villeins had to work very hard, especially during harvest time.

An absent landlord

'We don't actually see that much of the lord. He owns lots of manor houses and lots of land. He only comes to visit occasionally. We have much more to do with his steward. The steward is paid to get as much money as possible from the farm at each manor.'

Work without pay!

'We have to work on the manor farm, or the 'demesne' as it's called. I have to do three days work a week and an extra day during the Harvest. The rest of the week I work for myself to feed my family. Some people pay money to the lord instead of doing his work.'

Taxes, taxes and more taxes!

'There are lots of extra payments we have to make to the lord. For example, we pay a tax called 'merchet' if one of our daughters wants to get married. Sometimes, when his daughter is getting married or his son's becoming a knight then we have to pay an extra tax to help the lord to pay for it all.'

Hand over your animals!

'When one of us villeins dies the lord always takes his best animal for himself and gives the second best animal to the priest. Now that's a bit hard because I've only got one ox and two pigs. So when I go my son will be left with one pig. That's not all, my son will have to pay a tax called 'the entry fine' before he's allowed to take over the family farm.'

Runaways in chains!

'We can't leave the village and live elsewhere without the lord's permission. Sometimes villeins run away to get better jobs in the town. The lord's men always try to track them down. If they're caught, runaway slaves are brought back to the village in chains.'

Hands off, even if you're hungry!

'The lord loves to go hunting and the woods are full of wild animals. We're not allowed to hunt, even when we're really hungry. If you're caught poaching you can be fined or locked up. There's a dovecote on the manor where pigeons live. Only the lord and lady are allowed to eat them. They're a real nuisance because they eat our grain but we can't touch them.'

Use the lord's mill or else!

'The lord owns the mill where everybody has to go to grind the corn into flour. Every time you go there you have to hand over some of your grain to his miller as a payment. Some people try to beat him by having their own little hand mills at home. But if you get caught grinding your own corn you're in trouble.'

No silk for you, you're a villein!

'There are laws about what clothes we can wear and what clothes richer people can wear. As villeins we're not allowed to wear clothes made from expensive cloth or animal furs. Only the richer folk like the lord and his lady are allowed to wear fine clothes.'

---

1 In your own words write three short paragraphs about what it was like to be a villein. Use this writing frame to help you:

Lords got rich by making villeins poor. They did this in several ways _____
_____
_____

Villeins did not have the same rights as lords. We see this in the way _____
_____
_____

We don't know what most villeins thought about their lords but we can make a good guess. My guess is that _____

Did chivalry make life better?

In Hollywood films, rich lords and knights often treat poor people well. They follow a set of rules known as 'chivalry'. Did this really happen? Let's find out.

The rules of chivalry: The Hollywood version

◆ A knight must always be loyal to his lord.

◆ Knights must fight fairly and must treat all prisoners with respect.

◆ Knights should help anyone in trouble, especially poor defenceless people.

One historian has been trying to find out if knights really followed these rules of chivalry. He has looked at all the descriptions that survive of battles in England between 1066 and 1250. These are some of his findings:

Knights risked their own lives to save their lords from danger.

Knights often acted bravely if their lord was in danger. In 1191 William des Preaux saved King Richard the Lionheart in a battle by pretending that he was the king and allowing the enemy to chase him instead of Richard. When a great lord lost his horse during a battle it was expected that one of his knights would give up his own horse. This was very dangerous because without a horse a knight could be killed. During the Battle of Hastings, William the Conqueror's horse was killed. Eustace of Boulogne immediately got off his horse and gave it to William, risking his own life.

Did knights like this follow the rules of chivalry?

In a typical battle knights were careful not to injure each other.

In 1119, the English and French kings fought a battle in Normandy at a place called Bremule. There was fierce fighting and both sides were desperate to win. But, strangely, only three knights were killed.

In 1217, there was a battle between French and English armies at Lincoln. An English commander ordered his cross-bow men to shoot only at the horses of the enemy knights so that the knights would not be killed.

Knights often executed enemy foot-soldiers and cross-bow men.

Infantry soldiers were much poorer men than the knights themselves. Sometimes they were villeins. Knights seem to have particularly disliked enemy cross-bow men and archers. If cross-bow men were taken prisoner they were often executed after the battle. When King John captured Rochester Castle he spared the enemy knights but executed enemy cross-bow men. We also know that Henry III beheaded over three hundred enemy archers after a battle in 1264.

Knights sometimes killed villeins to show how strong they were.

Poor villeins were often caught up in war. While castles were difficult to capture it was easy to attack undefended villages and people with no weapons. It was common for knights to burn the houses and farms of ordinary villeins living on the land of the enemy lord. This led to famine and starvation. Sometimes knights went further and deliberately killed poor country people. During the 'Harrying of the North' in 1069, thousands of ordinary people were killed by Norman knights.

---

1 What evidence is there that knights obeyed or broke the rules of chivalry? Divide your page up with two headings:

Evidence that knights obeyed the rules	Evidence that knights broke the rules

2 In your own words summarise what you have learnt about how knights really behaved.

Medieval people were often very poor and did not have enough to eat. Today the government helps people who have no money. In medieval times the government did nothing to help the poor. Instead, rich people and the Church were expected to give charity to the local poor. Did they look after people in reality?

Great lords, bishops and monasteries each had someone called an almoner whose job it was to give 'alms' or charity to the poor. One 13th century book gives details about what a good almoner should do:

'He should give help to those who are old or sick. He should visit them frequently. He should listen calmly to all the loud cries for help from the poor and give help to all as far as he is able. He should not strike the poor or even shout at them, always remembering that the poor are made in the image of God.'

Many rich people did try to help the poor. Records survive that show how much medieval kings gave to charity. Edward I, for example, gave help to 700 poor families every week. He gave more at the time of great religious festivals. At Christmas in 1299 he gave 4000 poor families gifts of money or food. He also helped other people who needed support such as poor students who wanted to go to college.

An almoner's job was to look after the poor or sick.

Priests often criticised the rich for not giving enough. These two extracts come from the sermons of 14th century priests. Sermons like this were read out in church to encourage people to give more generously:

'The rich and greedy let their wealth rot in chests. They see the poor dying of hunger but they are unwilling to spend any of their money to save them. They have so many sets of clothes that many are never worn and get eaten by moths. And yet they will not give one old suit of clothes to the poor when they see them dying of cold in the winter.'

'The wealthy lords care more for their hunting dogs than they do for poor people. The poor are often so hungry that they would eat anything. Dogs will not accept any meat except the best. Sometimes the dogs' left over food is gathered up and given to the poor. It should be the other way around. These lords love their dogs and hate their fellow humans. Many people have starved to death but no hunting dogs are ever allowed to starve.'

A historian called Christopher Dyer has looked at church records to see how generous the Church was in reality. Let's look at some of the information that Christopher has discovered:

◆ Detailed records for looking after the poor survive from Beaulieu Abbey in 1270. Three times a week any left-over bread was given to the poor. The monks' old clothes were given away. When any of the abbey's animals died of disease, the meat of the dead animal was given as food to local sick people.

◆ On average monasteries gave about 2 per cent of their income away to the poor. We know a lot about Bolton Abbey in Yorkshire. The Abbey had an income every year of about £500. The almoner usually gave about £10 to the poor. However, at times of crisis, the Abbey reduced its charity. There was a terrible famine 1315-1318 and many people starved to death. During this crisis Bolton Abbey cut the money spent on charity from £10 a year to less than £2 a year.

◆ The single most generous member of the Church was a Bishop of Bath & Wells in the early 1300s. He made sure that 240 poor people were fed every day, and given new clothes once a year. He spent about 5 per cent of his income on the poor.

◆ Parish priests were supposed to give at least a quarter of their income to the poor. For most priests we have no detailed records. However, Christopher Dyer has found records for a very rich priest who lived in Bishop's Cleeve, in Gloucestershire, at the end of the 1300s. We know that he gave less than 1 per cent of his money to the local poor.

1 *What was an almoner? Explain in your own words what they were supposed to do.*

2 *Which one of the three following sentences describes what actually happened?*
   ◆ *The rich were always kind to the poor.*
   ◆ *The rich were sometimes kind and sometimes mean to the poor.*
   ◆ *The rich were never kind to the poor.*
   Explain your answer.

You are young villeins in a country village. You're sick of being bossed about by your lord. You're thinking about running away to a town. If you can live in a town for a year and a day you will become free and stop being a villein. However, there is a risk. The lord might come looking for you. If he catches you before the time is up, you will be punished. He will beat you and take you back to the village in chains. You will then have to pay a big fine. Is it worth the risk?

> **1** Work in a small group of three or four people. Look at the following information and decide whether, on balance, running away to a town is a good idea.

Will you be welcome in a town?

There are plenty of runaway villeins in towns. Towns are very unhealthy places and people die there more often than they do in the countryside. As a result there is always a need for new people. Without country people the towns would soon be empty.

Can you get a good job in a town?

There are plenty of jobs for labourers and servants. They have to work very hard and don't get much money. If you're lucky you will get a job as an apprentice. As an apprentice you get trained in a particular craft. After 7 years' training you will qualify as a craftsperson (like a cobbler, carpenter or blacksmith). Some tradespeople – like the grocers and the goldsmiths – are very well paid.

Where do people live?

If you get a job as a servant or an apprentice, you will live in the same house as your boss. The houses are very crowded. They are usually made of wood and often burn down. You will not have a room of your own. You may sleep in the workshop or share an attic room.

What were the guilds?

The craftspeople had societies called guilds. There were separate guilds for different crafts. They controlled prices and wages and made sure that work was of a good quality. They looked after their members in many ways. If people fell sick, for example, the guild would give them food and money. They also put on shows to entertain people on religious feast days.

Who were the powerful people in the town?

Most towns had a town council led by a mayor. He made important decisions about what happened in the town. Only rich men could sit on the council or become mayor. The mayor was chosen by other rich men in the town. Women were not allowed to take part. It was unusual for a man to move from a country village and get a top job as mayor.

Did people have fun in the towns?

People worked long hours but they had Sundays off and they did not work on some religious feast days. On these feast days there were shows for people to watch. There were alehouses but they closed very early. At night everyone had to be indoors before dark. This was called the curfew. You got in trouble if you went out after the curfew.

London was the biggest town in Britain, even in medieval times. London was busy, crowded and exciting. It was full of things to do and see. However, London could be unpleasant and even dangerous too. Would you have liked to live in London? Here's what two medieval people said:

Source 1: William Fitz Stephen was a Londoner who lived in the 1100s. He was very proud of his city. Let's see what he says about life in a medieval city:

Was London a pleasant place to live?

'Amongst the great and famous cities of the world, London is one of the most famous. Of all cities in the world it is the richest. The houses outside the town walls have large beautiful gardens, planted with trees. London has many excellent springs; the water is sweet, clear, and healthy. Holywell, Clerkenwell, and St Clement's well, are the most famous springs. Young people often meet at the springs when they go out to take the air in the summer evenings. The city is delightful indeed.'

Was there much to buy?

'There are plenty of wine-shops and places to eat. You can buy meat of every kind: roast, fried and boiled. There is coarse meat for the poor and more delicate meat for the rich, such as venison and small birds. If friends turn up unexpectedly you can always rush to the shops at the riverside and buy what you need for a meal. Merchants bring their goods here by sea from every country in the world: gold from Arabia, spice and incense, palm oil from Babylon, precious gems from Egypt, furs from Norway and Russia, fine cloth from China, wine from France.'

London was a big port in medieval times and lots of goods were transported by sea. In this picture, goods are being loaded onto boats.

What did Londoners do in their free time?

'Every year on Shrove Tuesday boys take fighting cocks into school. All morning is spent watching cock-fighting in the schoolrooms. Afterwards they go out into the fields and play football. Football is popular both with schoolboys and tradesmen. In summer, young men play also at jumping, archery, wrestling, stone-throwing, throwing the javelin and sword-fighting. Young girls spend their time dancing. In winter there is boar-fighting and bear-baiting to watch. When marsh land freezes, crowds of young men go skating on the ice. Some are experts and they have skates made from animal shinbones.'

... or a pain?

Source 2: An anonymous poet wrote a description of London in the 1400s. The poem is called London Lickpenny and it describes what happens when a man from the countryside visits the city. Let's see what the poet thought about life in London:

What happened when you arrived in London?

'Once in London, I made my way to Westminster to see a lawyer. I hoped he would help me with my case. When I found him, I said, "Have pity on a poor man. I'd like to give you silver but my purse is light." He would not help me, so for lack of money I cannot proceed.'

What was it like walking round London?

'As I pushed through the crowds I noticed that my hood had been stolen. By the time I noticed it wasn't worth stopping to look for it. Outside Westminster Hall there were many foreign traders. They tried to sell me all sorts of beautiful stuff, including fine felt hats and spectacles for reading. But for lack of money I could not buy.'

Was there anything to eat in London?

'At the city gates cooks called me over and tried to get me to eat. They showed me good bread, ale and wine. They spread out a table cloth and put fat ribs of beef on it. But for lack of money I could not eat. Other traders shouted to me "Ripe strawberries!" "Cherries on the branch". One urged me to buy some spice. He had pepper, saffron, clove and rice flour. But I could not buy.'

Did you stay in London?

'Finally I gave up, left the city and went into Kent. I went back to my life as a ploughman. God help you if you ever go to London. For in London he that lacks money shall not do well.'

---

1 Look at the two sources. Can you sum up each source in no more than one sentence?

2 Using the sources make two lists:

Good things about living in London	Bad things about living in London

3 Design a leaflet for travellers to medieval London. Try to come up with a balanced view of the good things and the bad things about London.

When we see a medieval town in a modern film it often looks like a very dirty, unhygienic place. Towns were certainly very crowded, but did this make them smelly? Medieval people did try to keep themselves and their streets clean, in different ways. Look at how they did this and then decide how smelly you think medieval towns really were.

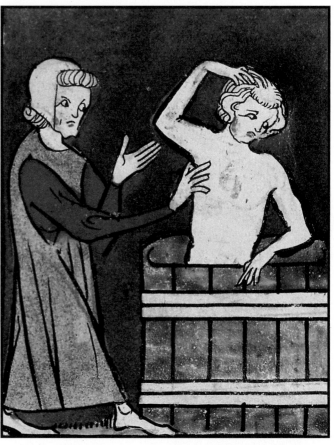

Some rich people would have had wooden bathtubs like the one shown here. In the picture a doctor looks at a man who is having a bath.

Dick Whittington and the toilets of London

In little villages getting rid of waste and filth was easy. In big towns it was much more difficult. People did try to keep their towns clean. In London, for example, there were several large public lavatories near the River Thames. Dick Whittingon, the hero of a pantomime story, really existed and was Lord Mayor of London. When he died he left money to build two enormous public lavatories on the banks of the Thames. One was for men and the other was for women. Each one had seating for 64 people. The waste went straight into the river and was washed away by the tide.

Emptying the cesspits

Some churches had public toilets and we have records written by the church wardens who looked after them. In one London church the cesspit (hole under the toilet) was cleaned out once every two years. Men called 'rakieres' did this dirty work, usually at night. They charged 24 pence for each ton of waste. In the records for this London church they were paid 120 pence – this means that they cleaned out five tons of waste from the pit.

Toilets and fatal accidents

Rich people had their own toilets (also known as 'privies'). In cellars and backyards there were often cesspits with wooden seats. One man called Richard le Rakiere was sitting on this kind of toilet when the rotten wood of the seat gave way. He fell into the cesspit and drowned.

Poor people often had no toilet or had to share one with many other families. The shortage of toilets could cause terrible accidents. In one case in London, a servant was sleeping in a room 30 feet above the road. He woke up in the night and needed to relieve himself. He went to the window in order to urinate but in his sleepy state he slipped and fell to his death.

Kings, toilets and baths

Many documents have survived showing how kings spent their money. At Dover Castle, Henry II spent a lot of money on a private toilet attached to his bedroom. He also made sure that there was piped water in different parts of the castle. Kings had a bath-man or 'ewerer', whose job it was to organise the king's washing. We know that King John's bath-man was paid a halfpenny a day and five pence every time the king had a bath. Since he was paid once every two weeks, we know that John had a bath once a fortnight.

Council rules and rubbish

Town councils introduced rules about how people should get rid of rubbish. Many of these town rules have survived. Some said that each family must get rid of its own rubbish and must not leave it on the street. As a result many families dug rubbish pits in their back yards or gardens. Some towns, including London, went further and had a street cleaning service. Butchers were fined if they did not get rid of any waste from their work.

A letter from the King

Despite these regulations streets were often filthy. In 1357, King Edward III travelled along the River Thames in London. He was so appalled by the smell that he wrote a letter to the Lord Mayor telling him to do something about it:

> The King to the Mayor and Sheriffs of our City of London, greeting.
>
> When passing along the water of the Thames, we have seen dung and rubbish and other filth piled up in several places. We have also noticed the fumes and other terrible smells resulting from this filth. From this there will great danger both to persons living in the city and to nobles and others travelling on the river. We, therefore, command you to clean the riverbanks, the streets and lanes of the city of all dung rubbish and other filth without delay. Anyone leaving dung or rubbish on the streets should be strictly punished so as cause fear and dread among others.

1 Make a list of all the ways in which medieval people tried to keep themselves and their towns clean.

2 Although people tried to keep them clean, do you think medieval towns were smelly?

3 In what ways was it easier for rich people to keep clean?

The strange science of medieval medicine

Medieval medicine was very different to modern medicine and to us it seems very strange. In this unit, find out how doctors worked in the Middle Ages. Start by looking at this unusual picture.

1 Imagine that you are working on an exhibition about medieval medicine. You have come across this odd picture. Can you guess what the doctors are doing?

2 Write a good caption for the picture explaining to the public what this picture is about.

Now look at this extra information and see if you can make more sense of the picture.

Medieval doctors took many ideas from the world of ancient Greece and Rome. Like the Greeks and Romans, they believed that every human body had four liquids inside it. These liquids were called humours. The four humours were:

◆ **Yellow bile**

◆ **Black bile**

◆ **Phlegm**

◆ **Blood**

Medieval doctors believed that people became ill because the body was producing too much of one of the humours.

To work out what was wrong with the humours, doctors looked at patients' urine. The colour of the urine showed whether the patient had too much of a particular humour. The study of urine was the main way of **diagnosing** (working out) what was wrong with a sick patient. Some very famous doctors did not bother to visit their patient. Their assistants collected urine samples and brought them to the doctor.

Doctors got rid of excess humours in a number of ways:

◆ By making people vomit.

◆ By making people go to the toilet.

◆ By cutting veins and letting people bleed.

3 Now write a better caption in your own words to go with the picture to explain to people visiting the exhibition what is happening.

The two years between 1348 and 1350 were some of the most terrifying years for people in Britain and Europe. A killer disease, called the Black Death, swept across the land. About a third of the people in Britain died from the illness. There was no cure. At the time nobody really knew what caused the Black Death. One medieval priest wrote, 'Everyone is terrified and no one knows what to do.'

The symptoms

The disease had horrible painful symptoms. Most of the people who caught it died after only three days. There was nothing that doctors could do for them.

◆ Huge boils, called buboes, appeared in their arm-pits and their groin. These buboes were as large as eggs or apples.

◆ The buboes then spread to other parts of the body.

◆ Painful black and red blotches appeared on the skin.

◆ The skin began to rot and smell.

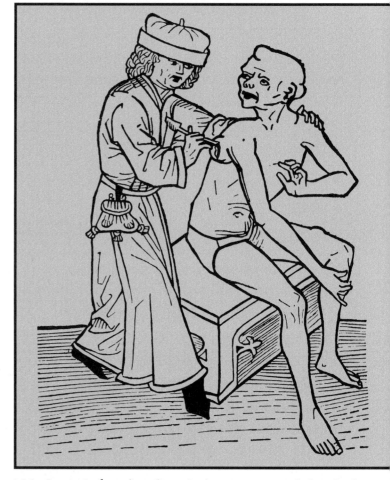

This doctor is *lancing* (bursting) an enormous buboe in the patient's armpit. Smelly black fluid squirted out of the buboe when it was burst. This helped to relieve the pain but was not a cure.

The death rate

The Black Death caused a lot of deaths. It was very easy to catch from somebody else who had it.

◆ Over a third of all people in Britain and Europe died of the Black Death.

◆ In some places many more than this died. For example, in Jarrow, Northumberland, 80 per cent of all the people in the village died.

◆ People of all ages died from the disease.

◆ Graveyards were soon too full. Big pits were dug outside towns where bodies were stacked on top of each other.

Did as many rich people die?

Throughout Europe there were many kings but only one king died of the Black Death. Most kings stayed in their castles to avoid the disease. King Alfonso of Spain was fighting a war when the disease broke out among his army. He stayed with them and soon died of the illness. Only one member of the English royal family died of the Black Death. She was Princess Joan, the daughter of King Edward III. Joan was travelling to France to marry a French prince when she fell ill and died.

Most rich people like Princess Joan did not catch the Black Death. They ate good food and their castles were cleaner than the ordinary houses.

1 Explain why people were so terrified of the Black Death. In you answer mention:

◆ why the symptoms were terrifying

◆ why the death rate was terrifying

◆ why thoughts about the causes were terrifying.

A rich man feasting with his family and servants. Did people like this have a better chance of escaping the Black Death?

What people thought caused the Black Death

Nobody at the time really knew what caused the Black Death. Many people were puzzled by the disease. They all had different ideas.

◆ Priests said that God caused the disease to punish people for being so wicked.

◆ Doctors believed it was because of astrology. They said that three evil planets (Saturn, Jupiter and Mars) had come together and this was upsetting the humours inside the human body.

We now know that the disease was carried by a few infected rats which came to Britain from Europe on sailing ships.

... The curse of the Black Death

A terrifying choice

Most people at the time had many friends and relatives who caught the Black Death. They had to make a very difficult decision. If they stayed with a victim, they might catch the disease. If they stayed away, their friends and relatives died a miserable, lonely death.

Now let's find out what medieval people did. We can do this by looking at the writing of an Italian man called Boccaccio (pronounced 'Bokatchio'). He lived through the Black Death in the city of Florence and later wrote an account of it:

This picture shows the mass burial of Black Death victims.

'Those who lived became very frightened. Most made a selfish decision: they tried to get away from the sick to save themselves.'

'Some shut themselves up in houses where no one had been sick. They tried to eat healthy food. They refused to speak to anyone who had been near the sick.'

'Others spent their time getting drunk and having wild parties. They went from tavern to tavern, drinking huge amounts of wine. Sometimes they entered other strangers' houses and helped themselves to anything inside.'

'People ignored sick members of their own families. People were so terrified that brothers and sisters refused to help other members of the family. Husbands and wives left each other to die and mothers and fathers abandoned their children. Only a few servants stayed with the sick for very high wages.'

2 What did the people of Florence do to avoid catching the Black Death?

3 You're a poor villein living in the countryside. Write a paragraph describing what you would do if your family caught the disease.

The survivors of the Black Death: a happy ending?

Overall, about 35 per cent of the population died of the Black Death in less than a year. For the survivors of the disease there were some benefits. In what ways did the Black Death make life better?

The Black Death was clearly a terrible tragedy. Because so many people died, there were lots of changes to life after the disease had gone. It may seem strange, but some historians think that there was also a good side to the Black Death. They say that life got better for the ordinary people who survived.

Before the Black Death

◆ The countryside was overcrowded with people. The rents paid to lords were very high. Many people had tiny farms or no land at all. If the harvest was very bad they starved to death.

◆ There were many people who were desperate for work. They would do jobs for very low wages just to get some money.

◆ Women found it particularly hard to get work. Lords and other bosses were men and they gave the best jobs to men. Women were paid less even when they did the same job as a man.

Changes after the Black Death

◆ There were fewer people and there was plenty of land to share. Rents paid to lords went down and the size of farms increased. With more land farmers grew more food for themselves and there was less risk of starvation.

◆ There was a shortage of workers. Lords had to pay more if they wanted workers, otherwise the workers would go to work for a different boss. So, wages went up and workers had more money to spend.

◆ There were more opportunities for women who wanted to do paid work. Lords needed workers badly and they realised that they needed to make more use of women workers. Some women were now able to get the same pay as men.

---

4 Look at each of the changes to life after the Black Death. Decide for each one whether it indicates life getting better or worse for ordinary people. Explain your answer.

Now look at this picture which shows peasants in the years after the Black Death relaxing by going on an organised rabbit hunt. With more food, lower rents and higher wages, country people had more time to spend on what they saw as fun activities. Are they wearing rags or good quality clothing? They are poaching rabbits on the lords' land but they don't seem to be trying to hide what they are doing. Do they look frightened about being caught by their lord?

After the Black Death villeins had more money and did not have to work so hard. They had more time to spend enjoying themselves. Here, well dressed, well fed peasants defy their lord by hunting.

1 Put yourself in the position of one of the peasants in the picture. Explain how your life has changed for the better since the Black Death.

2 Not everybody was happy with these changes. Can you suggest who might not have liked these changes and why?

was everybody happy?

You have probably guessed that the king and the lords were not so happy when life got better for the ordinary people. They didn't have as much power over the villeins as they used to have. And they had to pay the villeins more for their work. The king and the lords tried to get their power back by passing laws. Do you think they succeeded?

---

3 Your job is to use the sources:
   ◆ to find out more about the changes
   ◆ to look for evidence that some people were unhappy with the changes.

Source 1:

The lords and the king met in an emergency meeting of parliament in 1349. They made a new law called the *Statute of Labourers*. This is an extract from the new law.

> 'Because a great part of the people, especially workers and servants, died in the plague, some people will no longer work unless they receive excessive wages. Such increases in wages are not allowed. Workers must only receive the wages they were paid before the plague.'

Source 2:

This was written by John Gower. He was a lord who owned a lot of land He wrote this in 1375. It shows that the *Statute of Labourers* did not improve things and wages kept rising.

> 'The world goes from bad to worse. Wages are so high that a lord must now pay three times as much in wages as he used to do. In the good old days workers were happy to eat cheap corn bread. Now they eat the finest wheat bread. In the past a little cheese and milk seemed like a feast to them. Now they eat like lords, while we are facing ruin.'

The Peasants' Revolt

In June 1381, there was an outbreak of violence in Essex and Kent. Villeins and townsfolk in places such as Bury St Edmunds, Rochester and Maidstone gathered together. They murdered rich people and destroyed their property. This was the start of the Peasants' Revolt.

1 Using what you now know about the hardships of medieval life, can you think of any reasons why the peasants and townsfolk rebelled in 1381?

2 Look at this description of some of the violence in Bury St Edmunds and see if you can find any clues.

'The mob stormed everywhere, destroying the houses and property of any rich men and lawyers. They beheaded Lord John Cavendish, one of the king's leading judges. They placed his head in the market place of Bury St Edmunds. They also captured their landlord, the prior of the abbey of Bury St Edmunds and cruelly put him to death. His headless body was stripped and left in an open field for five days because no one dared to carry him away for fear of the fury of the country people. The mob entered the town of Bury, carrying the prior's head on a lance. To make fun of the prior and John Cavendish, they held together the two heads on the tops of lances as if they were kissing each other.'

3 Look at some information about their victims in Bury St Edmunds and see if you can work out any reasons why these men were hated so much.

The victims of the violence in Bury St Edmunds

Lord John Cavendish, Chief Justice of England

Lord John Cavendish was one of the country's chief judges. There was a great shortage of workers because of the Black Death. Those who were left demanded higher wages. A law was brought in saying that no one should have a pay rise. Judges, like Lord John Cavendish, went round the country to check that this law was being obeyed. Workers who asked for a pay rise were fined or imprisoned by the judges.

BEHEADED BY THE REBELS

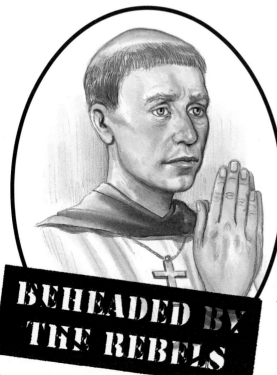

Prior John Cambridge, Bury St Edmunds Abbey

The prior was in charge of money matters in the Abbey. Abbeys like the one in Bury St Edmunds owned lots of land and controlled many villeins. After the Black Death there were fewer villeins to work on the abbey farms. Prior Cambridge insisted that all the surviving villeins should work extra hard to make up for those who had died. Many villeins expected to be treated better now that there were fewer workers. Prior Cambridge disagreed; he said that villeins had no rights and must do as they were told.

BEHEADED BY THE REBELS

Death at the Tower of London

The peasants of Kent and Essex marched to London. They joined forces with many poor people in the city. The peasants' leader was a man called Wat Tyler from Kent. Tyler and his followers terrorised the city of London for three days. What did they want?

Richard II, the young king, and his advisers did not know what to do. Richard met the peasants and tried to win them over by promising that he would make them free men, but they still refused to go home.

Meanwhile, one group of peasants burst into the Tower of London. There were many people inside the Tower but they singled out the Archbishop of Canterbury and the King's Treasurer. The peasants dragged these men outside the Tower and beheaded them. Their heads were put on poles and paraded through the streets. The heads were then placed on London Bridge for all to see. Why did the rebels hate the Archbishop of Canterbury and the King's Treasurer so much?

Simon Sudbury (the Archbishop of Canterbury) and Roger Hales (the Treasurer of England) were both beheaded by the peasants during the revolt.

Simon Sudbury: the Archbishop of Canterbury

BEHEADED BY THE REBELS

As well as being a leading churchman, Simon Sudbury was the Chancellor of England. This was a top government job similar to the prime minister's job today. Since King Richard II was only 14-years-old, Simon Sudbury played a big part in running the country. In 1381, England was at war with France, and the French were winning. The war was costing lots of money in taxes, which had to be paid by the ordinary people.

Roger Hales, Treasurer of England

BEHEADED BY THE REBELS

Roger Hales was in charge of the government's money matters. The government had run out of money to pay for the war in France. Roger Hales had to keep putting taxes up. In 1377 and 1379 the government introduced a heavy new tax, known as the 'poll tax'. These did not bring in enough money and another poll tax was imposed at the end of 1380. In 1381 Roger Hales sent tax collectors across the country to get the extra money.

> 1 Explain in your own words who Simon Sudbury and Roger Hales were and why you think the rebels hated them so much.

The end of the Revolt

The day after the killing at the Tower, King Richard met the rebels again. This meeting took place at Smithfield, the site of a market for farm animals. Wat Tyler rode up to the king and insulted the king and his friends. One of the companions of the king was the Lord Mayor of London, William Walworth. The mayor lost patience with Tyler and attacked him. Wat Tyler was knocked from his horse and another of the king's friends stabbed him to death.

The death of Tyler was a great turning point in the story of the Peasants Revolt. The rebels were stunned by the death of their leader and they seem to have lost the will to carry on. The king's soldiers surrounded the rebels and forced them to lay down their arms. They were allowed to leave London. However, in the weeks that followed the king's men tracked down the leaders of the Revolt and executed them. The king announced that all the promises of freedom made during the Revolt were worthless. In a message to the rebels of Essex, he said, ' Villeins you are and villeins you shall remain.'

Wat Tyler is killed. The king then rides over and tells the rebels to go home.

Hostile witnesses

Almost all the descriptions that we have of the Peasants' Revolt were written by enemies of the peasants. This description of the killing at the Tower was written by Thomas Walsingham, a monk of St Albans. His own abbey was attacked by the rebels and he was very hostile towards them.

'Who can believe it? Inferior country people dared to enter the bedroom of the king and the bedroom of the king's mother waving their dirty sticks. They dared to touch several most noble knights with their rough and filthy hands. These arrogant people sat on the king's bed and made jokes there. Some even asked the king's mother for a kiss. Amazingly the royal knights and squires did nothing to stop them.'

2 What would the story of the Peasants' Revolt be like if it was told from the point of view of the peasants? We know that at least one of the peasants' leaders could read and write. He was a priest called John Ball. After the rebellion he was captured. Put yourself in his position. Before you are executed you want to write an account of the Revolt from your point of view. Make sure you include:

◆ what caused the Revolt

◆ what happened during the Revolt.

How hard was life?

Imagine that you are working for a film-maker who wants to make an adventure film set in the Middle Ages. She wants to show the reality of life in the medieval world. She says, 'I don't understand what life was like for ordinary people in the Middle Ages. Was it hard or was it a good life? In some films you see folk in alehouses having a good time and dancing round maypoles. In other films the poor are treated like slaves by the rich. Which of these interpretations is correct?'

1 Look back at your work so far and make brief notes of any evidence of hardship and any evidence that life was good for ordinary people. Put your notes on a table like this:

Medieval people playing a game like hockey.

Evidence that life was hard	Evidence that life was good

2 Use your notes to produce a brief report for the film-maker answering the question 'How hard was life for medieval people in town and country?' Give the film director some advice on what aspect of life in the Middle Ages would be a good setting for an adventure film. You could suggest:

 ◆ the story of a peasant who runs away from a village to a town in search of a better life

 ◆ the story of someone who lives through and survives the Black Death

 ◆ the story of a peasant who gets caught up in the events of the Black Death.

3 Write the opening scene of the script for your chosen film. Make sure that you include lots of accurate detail based on the work you have done on how ordinary people lived in medieval times.

Index

Index

Acknowledgements

Every effort has been made to contact the holders of copyright material but if any have been inadvertently overlooked the Publishers will be pleased to make the necessary arrangements at the first opportunity.

The Publishers would like to give special thanks to Mel Gibson and Icon Productions.

Photographs

The Publishers would like to thank the following for permission to reproduce photographs on these pages:

T = top, B = bottom, C = centre, L = left, R = right

Cover image: By permission of the British Library, MS Roy 2 OCVII f. 133.

AKG London, 65; Art Archive, London, 35, 79, 110; Art Resource, New York, 34; Bibliothèque nationale de France, Paris, 5L, 5R, 36, 59T, 59C, 59B, 94–95; Bibliothèque royale Albert Premier, Brussels, 102; Bodleian Library, Oxford, 37, 57, T, 57C, 57B, 68; 'BRAVEHEART'© 1995 Twentieth Century Fox Film Corporation. All rights reserved. 48; Bridgeman Art Library, London, 51T, 51B, 72, 73T, 73B, 83, 87T, 87B; British Library, 29, 32, 40, 45, 54, 75, 77B, 86, 90, 96, 98, 101, 108, 109; CADW: Welsh Historic Monuments. Crown Copyright (illustration by Terry Ball), 47; English Heritage, London, 46, 74, 77T, 78; Glasgow Museums: The Burrell Collection, 104; Mary Evans Picture Library, London, 64; Michael Holdford (photographic copyright), 6, 7, 10, 11T, 11B, 13, 14, 15T, 15B, 16, 17, 18, 22; The Master and Fellows of Corpus Christi College, Cambridge, 26T, 26R, 26C, 26L; St. John's College, Cambridge, 58; St. Peter's Church, Marlow, 66; York Archaeological Trust, 82; World Health Organisation, Geneva, 100.

Artwork

The Publishers would like to thank the following for permission to reproduce artwork on these pages:

Osprey Publishing Ltd, Oxford, 18-19 from **ELITE 9** *The Normans*, Plate C, by Angus McBride, 20 from **WARRIOR I** *Norman Knight*, Plate K, by Christa Hook, 21 from **WARRIOR 1** *Norman Knight*, Plate J, by Christa Hook, 25 from **WARRIOR 1** *Norman Knight*, Plate I, by Christa Hook, 28 from **WARRIOR 1** *Norman Knight*, Plate C, by Christa Hook, 38 from **MAA III** *The Armies of Crécy and Poitiers*, Plate A, by Christopher Rothero, 44 from **ELITE 9** *The Normans*, Plate F, by Angus McBride, 80 from **ELITE 9** *The Normans*, Plate E, by Angus McBride, 88 from **WARRIOR 1** *Norman Knight*, Plate L, by Christa Hook.

All other artwork by Peter Bull